Book Series # 1

A Devotional for Understanding and Acceptance

Volume 2

April through June 2023

A Devotional Series

by

Dr. Jay Newman

 Jay Newman is a founding partner of Culture by Choice™, a company that focuses on helping clients create the culture they desire by determining what exists now, who the people are that make up that existing culture, and then creating the coaching processes needed to move the company from where they are to where they want to be. Jay received his Doctorate in Education Leadership from Vanderbilt University in 1984. Jay spent over 35 years in public education teaching Biology and Chemistry and then moving into the administrative ranks. When he retired from education in 2006, he left having served his final 8 years as the County Superintendent of Schools in St. Joseph County Michigan. He returned to the superintendency in 2013-14 for a one-year interim position with the Colon Community Schools in Michigan.

Jay and his wife Barb attended Augustana College in Rock Island, Illinois. While at Augustana, Jay had several professors that had a lasting impact on his thinking and faith. Some of these were teachers of Religion, while others were coaches and teachers in Science, Math, and History. Jay had several friends who attended the seminary after college, while Jay went into public education. Jay's faith was critical in his decision-making and career trajectory. Teaching Biology and Chemistry and later going into the administrative ranks, Jay stayed true to his Christian Faith. He challenged the status quo in education and looked for answers beyond traditional school textbooks. Believing that the best knowledge is knowledge that can withstand critical arguments, he was always open to discussing a variety of topics. Among these were evolution, quantum Physics, Environmental Sciences, and leadership.

Jay and Barb have been active members of the United Methodist Church for over 50 years and even though there has been a great deal of controversy in the church over the past decade or two, they do not see these issuers as impinging upon their faith. All of the controversy should be left to God, and we Christians should just fulfill Christ's two great commandments: Love God with all your being and love your fellow human beings as Jesus loved us.

A synopsis of this Series

Book series # 1is titled **A Devotional for Understanding and Acceptance**. In the works is a second series that will be titled **A Devotional for the Love of God**. I have not yet pondered the third in this series of books. Each series will be four books, with each book comprising the Daily Devotionals I have written for each year. Series # 1 was completed during 2023 and Series # 2 is planned for 2024. Volume 2 for Series # 1 covers April 1 through the end of June 2023. I hope you enjoy this series and even more, I hope you find inspiration to live a life filled with the Love of Christ.

Some of the topics might seem to be controversial for some people, but my intention is always to share my sense of God's Love as it has been shared with me. Paramount in my intentions is the simple fact that as Christians we already know that we cannot earn our way to heaven. If we could earn our way to heaven, there would have been no need for Christ to come to Earth and be sacrificed for our salvation. With that in mind, it should also be acknowledged that, if we cannot earn our way to heaven, we cannot facilitate the entrance into heaven for any other person by any means than simply sharing God's Love and encouraging them to accept Christ as their savior while, in turn, sharing God's Love with all they encounter as well.

Should you find this book and others in the series to be useful in your faith journey, feel free to contact me and let me know. How we discover Christ and invite him into our lives is not as important as the simple act of doing so. I encourage all people everywhere to really investigate the promise of Jesus and the peace and love he will bring into your life when you simply turn your life over to him. Grace, Peace, and Love to all! AMEN!

Day 91: A Devotional for Understanding and Acceptance

The day before Palm Sunday, is traditionally thought of as Lazarus Day, or the day Jesus brought Lazarus back from the dead! Jesus performed many miracles but the most amazing was raising Lazarus from his tomb, 4 days after he had died. The compassion of Christ is truly an amazing precursor to the passion for humanity he displayed by allowing himself to be crucified as a sacrifice for our sins. Some people still don't get it. For some reason they think it is all either a hoax or Jesus allowed this to happen to show how all people should obey laws that allow us to hate those who are different! (race, skin color, language, health or financial status, political philosophy, or even different concept of God or Salvation!) Jesus made the sacrifice for the Salvation of ALL!

Luke 15:3-4 So he told them this parable: "What man of you, having a hundred sheep, if he has lost one of them, does not leave the ninety-nine in the open country, and go after the one that is lost, until he finds it?

When he brought Lazarus from the dead after 4 days, he was telling every single human being on Earth that no one, not a single solitary soul, was beyond his reach for salvation. It's time to stop the Hatred, the sorting and selecting, the killing, destroying, condemning, and ridiculing! It's an abomination, especially in this Easter Season! Only God and his chosen first born and only Child have the purity of heart and level of compassion to Judge.

"Do not judge, or you too will be judged. For in the same way you judge others, you will be judged, and with the measure you use, it will be measured to you. "Why do you look at the speck of sawdust in your brother's eye and pay no attention to the plank in your own eye? Matthew 7:1-3

"Amazing Grace, how sweet the sound, that saved at wretch like me, I once was lost but now am found, was blind but now I see!"

My Prayer: **Dear Jesus forgive our constant desire to Judge. Who among us would have entered Lazarus tomb to raise him from death! I dare say 99+% of us would never have entered that tomb. You mastered death and offer the way to salvation to ALL. ALL means ALL, not just those we agree with. Let us not forget that. It's not our place to decide! It's not** the place for politicians, priests, rabbis, Popes, or media talking heads. That is the job that only Jesus, under your watchful loving eye, has earned the right to hold! AMEN

Day 92: A Devotional for Understanding and Acceptance

Nearly 2000 years ago, this is what happened as told in the Gospels of Luke and Matthew. Just a day before Jesus had raised Lazarus from his tomb. Word spread and the leaders of the Jewish Temple in Jerusalem and the local Roman Governor, were very agitated. Who was this guy?

"Go to the village ahead of you, and as you enter it, you will find a colt tied there, which no one has ever ridden. Untie it and bring it here. If anyone asks you, 'Why are you untying it?' say, 'The Lord needs it.'"

Those who were sent ahead went and found it just as he had told them. As they were untying the colt, its owners asked them, "Why are you untying the colt?" They replied, "The Lord needs it." They brought it to Jesus, threw their cloaks on the colt and put Jesus on it. As he went along, people spread their cloaks on the road. When he came near the place where the road goes down the Mount of Olives, the whole crowd of disciples began joyfully to praise God in loud voices for all the miracles they had seen:

"Blessed is the king who comes in the name of the Lord!"

"Peace in heaven and glory in the highest!"

Some of the Pharisees in the crowd said to Jesus, "Teacher, rebuke your disciples!"

"I tell you, "He replied, "if they keep quiet, the stones will cry out." Luke: 19:30-42 A very large crowd spread their cloaks on the road, while others cut palm branches from the trees and spread them on the road Matthew 21:2

And so, the beginning of the end, which created a whole new beginning for mankind, was launched.

My Prayer: Gracious Lord, thank you for your sacrifice. This Easter is an opportunity to renew our dedication to the principles of love and compassion that were the cornerstone of early Christianity. Help us value human life more than anything else. That must become our priority. We know that, from time to time, we have to make some very difficult decisions. Those decisions should be made by the people most affected by those decisions. Bless your people with your love and abundance. When we place our faith in you, nothing is impossible. AMEN

Day 93: A Devotional for Understanding and Acceptance

Holy Monday is observed annually on the day after Palm Sunday. It commemorates Jesus's life, faith, and the events leading up to his death and eventual resurrection. According to the Bible, Holy Monday is the day after Jesus was greeted with palm leaves, onlookers lain their cloaks on the path as Jesus and his disciples proceeded towards Jerusalem, and the day before Judas decided to betray him.

For Christians, the holiday is the beginning of the Holy Week preparation, which includes reading the Bible and reflecting on the Scripture.

Why is this a significant point in the Passion of Christ? The very deserved adulation of Jesus, based on his love and compassionate care and concern for everyday people angered the Priests, Pharisees, Sadducee's, and especially upset the Roman Regional Government! Each of these appointed, or born leaders thought that they deserved adulation because of who they were. People adored Jesus because of the Love he freely shared and compassion he openly showed for everyone. No every had to earn it nor could they ever do so. When we truly emulate Jesus we run the risk of being despised for the love and compassion we share!

Politicians will try to destroy us. Religious establishment will ridicule us! Haters will hate us! We will be misunderstood and be accused of being naive! BUT THE REWARD IS AN ETERNAL HOME WITH ALL THAT IS WONDERFUL AND GOOD AND HOLY!

My Prayer: Holy Lord and Savior, Jesus Christ, we thank you for letting us, common people, nobodies, rejected by the rich and powerful, marginalized, looked down upon, those of us who don't clearly speak the way everyone expects us to! You have given us an easy set of rules to follow: 1)Love God, 2) Love each other, 3) Do this Always—Forever and Ever! AMEN

THANK YOU: All my readers-

Day 94: A Devotional for Understanding and Acceptance

What's all this talk about "WOKE?" I woke up this morning, and you know what? I am very glad I did! If I had not "woke up" this morning, I would have missed a great deal. You know what? There are a lot of people who hope we will sleepwalk through our days. They hope we will not realize how much they are trying to keep from us. They think they know secrets and that if it gets out, we will be able to figure out the secrets to huge successes that depend on us not knowing what they are doing? They've become so good at it that they have hoodwinked us into believing that anyone who wants to share the secrets to an amazing life must be from the devil himself. That's exactly what the leaders, rich people, those who wanted to control the minds of the masses accused Jesus of 2,000 years ago. The High Priest, Pharisees, Sanhedrin, The Rome appointed King Herod and Governor Pilate; all saw Jesus as someone who could awaken too many people and that was exceedingly dangerous.

Things have not changed much in 2,000 years. Jesus and his disciples are still sharing the message of Love and the world is still in continuous rebellion. What is the world rebelling against? The simplicity of the answer! Love is the only answer! Not power; not might; not conformity; not legalism; not war; not hatred; not debate; no, nothing can deny the incredible power of God's Love.

That is where we must begin. Spreading God's Love to all ends of Creation. To begin anywhere else is not supported in any passage of the Gospels. "Until we accept Christ" is not a call to violent action. "Until we accept Christ" is a loving act of our own free will and can only be a voluntary action each person commits to our love and devotion to a loving God and Savior! Judas tried to force Jesus into pushing the matter into a violent revolution against the authorities of the day! That would have only driven more of the world away from true acts of Love and Kindness. If God's Love can only be established through violence, that's not Love at All!

My Prayer: Gracious God, we've been wandering in the wilderness again! As soon as we begin to understand, we fall for the false promises of the world and a hope for domination. We can't make every person in this world comply. But we can, each one of us, Share Your Love and Your Promise of Salvation! Anyone who have been bullied knows that they may comply, for a while, but they do not willingly give their heartfelt Live to that bully. Help us remember 1 Corinthians verses 4-8 as the description of Love you shared with us and wish us to share with others! AMEN

Day 95: A Devotional for Understanding and Acceptance

Just because you woke up, doesn't mean you paid attention. There are a great many people who seem like they are tuned in, but when we tune into their wavelength, all you hear is static. When people are focused on ideologies that are zeroed in on causing pain and suffering, you know they are tuned into the wrong wavelength. Positive wavelengths find the good in people and opportunities for growth. Negative, hurtful wavelengths look for what's wrong with others and look to limit the opportunities of those they feel are unworthy.

What we need, truly need, is that which can give us Peace, (Glory to God in the highest, and on earth peace, good will toward men (Luke 2:14).) Love, and Joy. So why do we keep exhibiting behaviors that bring us just the opposite of Peace, Love, and Joy. Peace is a product of calmness, quietude, ease, cooperation, gentleness, and caring! Let's look at Love through its opposite, HATE! No one has ever hated their way into love! Jesus defines love as forgiveness (Therefore I tell you, many as her sins are, they are forgiven, for her love is great; whereas he to whom little is forgiven has but little love.") Luke 7:47, Mercy (*"Finally, all of you be of one mind, having compassion for one another; love as brothers, be tenderhearted, be courteous; not returning evil for evil or reviling for reviling, but on the contrary blessing, knowing that you were called to this, that you may inherit a blessing."* 1 Peter 3:8-9) truth, (Love does not rejoice in unrighteousness but rejoices with the truth" 1 Corinthians 13:6)and sacrifice (Greater love has no one than this: to lay down [sacrifice] one's life for one's friends. John 15:13) He tells us that we will be forgiven and shown mercy in the same measure we are willing to forgive others and show mercy. Not just to those we like and care for but in relation to those who have wronged us. The Beatles have been thought of as being Anti-Christian Faith, however, some of the last words written for a song by Lennon and McCartney were: "And in the End, The Love You Take, Is Equal to the Love you Make."

Finally, if we find Peace, we will see that it was generated through sharing Love; pure, unadulterated, unconditional LOVE. When have Peace and we experience God's Unconditional Love and share it freely, we will sense a level of Joy that will allow us to smile from our SOUL!

My Prayer for All of Humanity is this: Gracious God, teach us to be quiet, calm, and generous. Show us how to share love without questioning motives. Move our hearts so that we never again believe that we can fight our way to Peace, hate our way to God's Love, forcefully create a Joyful World. Create in us a true feeling of acceptance of where we are, as flawed as that may be, and accept those same flaws in others from a totally nonjudgmental reference point. And most importantly, let us see ourselves as being equals on all levels with every other human on planet Earth. The beauty of our existence is that "God so love the world, that he gave his only Child as a Sacrifice for our Salvation!" AMEN

Day 96: A Devotional for Understanding and Acceptance

Today is Maundy Thursday; Maundy is a shortened version of the Latin word Mandatum, which means mandate. Also thought of as Christ's Mandate. *"A new commandment I give to you, that you love one another: just as I have loved you, you also are to love one another"* John 13:34. It is believed that this new commandment was given to the disciples at Jesus last Passover Meal celebration. What Christians commonly refer to as the Last Supper.

Notice, Christ's Mandate is not about holding others accountable for their violations of "God's Law!" It is, very straight out *stated: "A new commandment I give to you, that you love one another: just as I have loved you, you also are to love one another."*

As we approach the day of Crucifixion, what we call "Good Friday," (one might wonder how a crucifixion can be Good), let's pray that Christians around the world will put Loving One Another above every other goal. There can be no freedom without Love. As long as our focus is on what people are doing wrong, rather than Loving others as Christ has loved us, we will be stuck in a judgmental mindset. Maundy Thursday is significant in that, even as Jesus knew he would soon be betrayed and crucified, he commanded his followers to Love; not condemn, but Love!

If we, as a Faith Community, are to ever to achieve the goals that Jesus set for us, our top priority must be to return to his command! If we Christians keep fighting with one another over doctrine and biblical interpretations, we do a huge disservice to Jesus. Please, everyone: STOP ARGUING and just follow Christ's New Commandment!

My Prayer: Gracious Lord Jesus, forgive us our failure to follow your New Commandment. I pray that All Christians, everywhere, will make the #1 priority **SHARING YOUR LOVE.** We very clearly see what happens when we would rather make others adhere to a set of laws that we have difficulty following ourselves. We pick out a few we think are the worst transgressions and make sure those violations are punished, but say those others really are so bad. In doing this, we marginalize people we should be seeking for the sake of Christ's sacrifice. We see the pain and suffering in our world today; War rages, weather is killing thousands through floods, droughts, excessive heat, avalanches, fires, and tornados. Help us realize that these are the products of HATE. Heal our world through your Amazing Grace and Love! AMEN, HALLELUJAH, AMEN,

Day 97: A Devotional for Understanding and Acceptance

Why just Good Friday? Why not **Amazing, Incredible, FANTASTIC FRIDAY?**

Jesus' life was, indeed, incredibly amazing. But the crucifixion was Good only because it was required for the resurrection that will come on the third day. The crucifixion and resurrection allowed Jesus to transition from a temporal body to spiritual entity capable of being separate from a physical form that experiences existence based on an awareness from a human perspective. Even though he always was very capable of demonstrating experiences beyond the common awareness of most humans, the reality was until they saw what was truly possible, they would, most likely, not believe what they saw. The miracles he performed provided evidence of this. Being capable of performing miracles did not mean his detractors would not question "By what power he performed them." If Jesus had demonstrated powers beyond the senses of human awareness, it most likely would have caused such a turn in the wrong direction.

Not many people acquire an ability to separate the self from the soul. From the first time Jesus interacted with the Rabbis at the Temple, he showed an awareness and understanding of the Torah than the average 12-year-old in Judaea during his day. He realized that he not only had an awareness of where his person was, but also where his spirit was. Jesus wanted us to understand that his kingdom was not of this world. With His Crucifixion, he not only demonstrated that he transcended the physical life but in 3 days he would show the Power of God's Spirit to overcome any and all trials, tribulations, and adversities. Jesus demonstrated that the body is just a body and can be destroyed by small people. But the soul is the true seat of energy, life, and power. Only God can destroy a soul and he decided to provide a choice to every human to either connect with Him in the Spirit through Christ or reject eternal life and allow it to wither like the fig tree that was not producing fruit.

Nearly 2,000 years ago Jesus was Crucified to save us through a choice given to us. Will we defend Christ's Love by Loving others unconditionally, thus providing fruit for generations yet to come! Or will we allow the spirit Christ placed in our hearts to wither like the fig tree that would not produce fruit. "Seeing a fig tree by the road, he went up to it but found nothing on it except leaves. Then he said to it, "May you never bear fruit again!" Immediately the tree withered." Matthew 21:19

My Prayer: Gracious God, who allowed his only Child to be Crucified for our Salvation, may we never take that sacrifice for granted. May we be eternally grateful for the chance we've been given to bear fruit that can lead many to your offer of eternal life. As has been sung in Churches around the world.

We are one in the Spirit; we are one in the Lord

We are one in the Spirit; we are one in the Lord

And we pray that our unity will one day be restored

And they'll know we are **Christians** by our **love**, by our **love**

Yeah, they'll know we are **Christians** by our **love**. **AMEN**

Day 98: A Devotional for Understanding and Acceptance

What do we call The Saturday before Easter. This is the day of the Easter Vigil. The Day Christians await the Resurrection. It has been called Easter Eve, Black Saturday, or Holy Saturday. In our modern Christian Liturgical Calendar, it is the last day of Lent. But the Disciples, and Jesus himself, were in quite a different Mental and Spiritual state than were the Christians who decided Pascha (the Greek word that is given to Easter) should be celebrated each year. Early Christians celebrated Easter at the same time as Passover, but on the Sunday following the Passover Sabbath.

For Jesus, who was Crucified the day before, it was time he spent in the Tomb. Though his body had been executed on a Roman Cross, his Spirit awaited the day after the Passover Sabbath, when on that the third day he had stated that the destroyed Temple would be raised. Though his body had ceased to live, he was fully aware of all that was happening. When we allow our inner spiritual ("Great I am") being to take precedence over our physical small ("I am") being, we have that out of body experience. When we read the Bible, we are confronted with many instances when Jesus and the Disciples demonstrated this ability. Jesus, because of the strength of his inner connection with God, his Parent, could stay in that state for extended periods of time. The Disciples, as is the case with most of us, came to their senses and lost Faith in that inner connection with God and found themselves, in a situation where Jesus needed to rescue them. Here is the most commonly thought of event.

Immediately Jesus made the disciples get into the boat and go on ahead of him to the other side, while he dismissed the crowd. After he had dismissed them, he went up on a mountainside by himself to pray. Later that night, he was there alone, and the boat was already a considerable distance from land, buffeted by the waves because the wind was against it.

Shortly before dawn Jesus went out to them, walking on the lake. When the disciples saw him walking on the lake, they were terrified. "It's a ghost," they said, and cried out in fear. But Jesus immediately said to them: "Take courage! It is I. Don't be afraid." "Lord, if it's you," Peter replied, "tell me to come to you on the water." "Come," he said.

Then Peter got down out of the boat, walked on the water and came toward Jesus. But when he saw the wind, he was afraid and, beginning to sink, cried out, "Lord, save me!" Immediately Jesus reached out his hand and caught him. "You of little faith," he said, "why did you doubt?"

And when they climbed into the boat, the wind died down. Then those who were in the boat worshiped him, saying, "Truly you are the Son of God." Matthew 14:22-33

As Jesus' body lay in the Tomb, he was not dead, as when we die, we are not dead either. Our bodies, cease to be supported by the biological systems that kept us physically "alive" but our inner being is still present and since Jesus' victory over Death, our spirits can reconnect with the Creator Spirit. The first act of Jesus Spiritual Being was to appear to all the dead souls of the world to let their spirits know of HIS victory over death.

"For this is the reason the gospel was preached even to those who are now dead, so that they might be judged according to human standards in regard to the body but live according to God in regard to the spirit." 1 Peter 4:6

My Prayer: Let us pray to Jesus, our Savior, that the Creator of all will allow our Spirits to explore their true essence and become the amazing spiritual beings we are intended to be. When we connect our inner being with the spirit of the Living God, we begin to see the potential we each have to Bring the Peace of our Lord and Savior, Jesus Christ, and the LOVE OF THE CREATOR OF ALL LIFE, to every corner and all ends of Creation. This is our purpose. Let us use the Spirit of this day, The (Paschal) Easter Eve Saturday to make our worldwide, focused effort to share The Good News and God's Amazing Gracious Love. When we focus on this purpose, no need will be unmet. No danger will befall us. To God be the Glory! **AMEN**

Day 99: A Devotional for Understanding and Acceptance

Easter Sunday! Hallelujah He is Risen! The World will never be the SAME! Go and Share the Good News! LOVE HAS TRIUMPHED over hate. Let's all act like it! Stop the hate filled actions! What are those? All the negative emotion driven, Destructive Behaviors. How do we do that? Here's an example of how to de-escalate our present reaction to the crises we see in our world today.

1-I am so angry with those people! 2- Replace 1 With: I feel so angry about how those people act! 3- Now replace 2 With: those actions are something that could make another person angry if they forget that Christ's final commandment was to love each other as he loved us! But as for me and my household; "We will never forget, for we serve the risen SAVIOR, Jesus Christ!

Easter has been abused as a reason to hate Jews! Many different organizations have taken that notion and applied that hate to persecute other groups which is very antithetical to the very reason Jesus needed to be Sacrificed! When will WE learn.

My Prayer: Oh, Great Redeemer Lord, teach us to apply the Prayer, You taught us. Our Father (Devine Parent) Who is in Heaven Holy is your Name (The Great I am) Your Kingdom Reigns, Your Will Is Established Here Today on this very Earth, As it is Already Applied in Heaven. Give us today and Every day the basics we need for life And Forgive our inadequate, Unloving Behaviors towards others As we Forgive those who have behaved badly and unloving toward us And lead us away from the Temptation to punish others, which is a judgment reserved for You Alone, Please, Deliver us from All of our own Evil Desires For It is Your Kingdom And It is Your Power And We should Glorify You Now and Forever AMEN! HALLELUJAH! AMEN!

Day 100: A Devotional for Understanding and Acceptance

After the Resurrection and before the Ascension, Jesus appeared to the Disciples and/or other followers at least 10 times over a 40-day period. Here is an amazing series of verses from Luke, Chapter 24:13-35: (THE ORIGINAL EMMAUS WALK)

"Now that same day two of them were going to a village called Emmaus, about seven miles from Jerusalem. They were talking with each other about everything that had happened. As they talked and discussed these things with each other, Jesus himself came up and walked along with them; but they were kept from recognizing him.

He asked them, "What are you discussing together as you walk along?"

They stood still, their faces downcast. One of them, named Cleopas, asked him, "Are you the only one visiting Jerusalem who does not know the things that have happened there in these days?"

"What things?" he asked.

"About Jesus of Nazareth," they replied. "He was a prophet, powerful in word and deed before God and all the people. The chief priests and our rulers handed him over to be sentenced to death, and they crucified him; but we had hoped that he was the one who was going to redeem Israel. And what is more, it is the third day since all this took place. In addition, some of our women amazed us. They went to the tomb early this morning but didn't find his body. They came and told us that they had seen a vision of angels, who said he was alive. Then some of our companions went to the tomb and found it just as the women had said, but they did not see Jesus."

He said to them, "How foolish you are, and how slow to believe all that the prophets have spoken! Did not the Messiah have to suffer these things and then enter his glory?" And beginning with Moses and all the Prophets, he explained to them what was said in all the Scriptures concerning himself. As they approached the village to which they were going, Jesus continued on as if he were going farther. But they urged him strongly, "Stay with us, for it is nearly evening; the day is almost over." So, he went in to stay with them.

When he was at the table with them, he took bread, gave thanks, broke it and began to give it to them. Then their eyes were opened, and they recognized him, and he disappeared from their sight. They asked each other, "Were not our hearts burning within us while he talked with us on the road and opened the Scriptures to us?"

They got up and returned at once to Jerusalem. There they found the Eleven and those with them, assembled together and saying, "It is true! The Lord has risen and has appeared to Simon." Then the two told what had happened on the way, and how Jesus was recognized by them when he broke the bread."

My Prayer: Gracious Lord Jesus, it is true! You overcame death and appeared to those who truly love you! They obeyed your commands and spread the Gospel. Everywhere they went, to the ends of the Earth as they knew it at the time. They spread without the power to punish, only the power to heal and share your love. Help us remember, we cannot change anyone out of fear, hate, or threat of violence. Love will conquer all, only if those who need our love receive it unconditionally. But God demonstrates his own love for us in this: While we were still sinners, Christ died for us. Romans 5:8–we are still sinners, not one of us is pure! **AMEN**

Day 101: A Devotional for Understanding and Acceptance

Why do things happen to me that are so contrary to what I would like to have happened for me? The best answer for this question is: You are what you think! You've heard it said before that You are what you eat! Let's examine what you eat. Do you eat things that you Don't Like? If you think you don't like it, will you try it? How many foods in your life have you not eaten because you thought you didn't like it? Everything you take into your body that is metabolizable gets either converted to energy to allow life processes to carry on, or becomes part of your body, (muscle, skin, tissue, organs, nerves, etc.) or is eliminated as waste. A few non-metabolizable materials can be stored in the liver, muscles, or fatty tissues and can cause long-term problems for us. Mercury, Lead, other heavy metals, pesticides, herbicides, plastics, other organic chemicals, all are being found to have long range negative effects on people. Sometimes we think what we are consuming is good for us, and most of the time we are right. But there are things that are in our food, occasionally, that are very harmful. We are what we think. If what we think about what we experience in the world leads us into a harmful place, somebody's going to get harmed. Either you or somebody else.

So back to the answer to today's devotional question. Why do things happen to me that are so contrary to what I would like to have happened for me? I have rarely found a person who is an unapologetic optimist who has run into trouble in their lives. These people seem to be the personification of turning lemons into lemonade. To the contrary, I do not ever remember an unabashed pessimist that has had a life that is smooth sailing for them and everyone around them. There are times when the gloom and doom folks make a lot of money and appear to be highly successful. But, when you examine the totality of the lives and the lives of those around them, you see chaos and horrible disasters in their wake! Thinking that resources are scarce, so I must get all I can to secure my future is how the disparity between the wealthy and the very poor has taken place. What did Jesus have to say about this?

"Then Jesus said to his disciples, 'Truly I tell you; it is hard for someone who is rich to enter the kingdom of heaven. Again, I tell you, it is easier for a camel to go through the eye of a needle than for someone who is rich to enter the kingdom of God.' When the disciples heard this, they were greatly astonished and asked, 'Who then can be saved?' Jesus looked at them and said, 'With man this is impossible, but with God all things are possible.' " Matthew 19:23-26 And: "No one can serve two masters. Either you will hate the one and love the other, or you will be devoted to the one and despise the other. You cannot serve both God and money." Matthew 6:24

My Prayer: Heavenly Creator God and Redeemer Christ Jesus, help us to not be people who fear that we will run out of money, and as a result worship money. Let us not think so much about money that we become so focused on money we either step all over people to get and keep all the money we can or become the people that the money worshippers have become so adept at convincing others that, even though they are walking all over us, they are doing it for our own good and that those people who say they want to help us are truly evil and want to keep us from being as free as they guarantee we will be! Help us put our faith and trust in **YOU and YOU ALONE!** All else is folly. Help us remember that evil knows no political party. It will use liberals, conservatives, moderates, or any other approach. Help us to always follow your 2 greatest commands! **LOVE GOD WITH ALL YOUR HEART, MIND, SPIRIT, ENERGY** and **LOVE EACH OTHER (all means all, not just your friends: even the truly godless do that) AS CHRIST HAS LOVED US!   AMEN-ALL GLORY, HONOR AND PRAISE TO YOU OUR PERSONAL GOD AND SAVIOR: AMEN**

This is an added Note!

At this point in the year, I began to question whether I truly had any followers of this devotional series. So, this post was designed to take the temperature of the following. The response I got was incredible and so I went forward with my writing. After this day 102 post, I will share some of the comments I received.

Day 102: A Devotional for Understanding and Acceptance

Should I continue with this Devotional? Please give an honest opinion. When I speak to a group on a regular basis, I can tell if the audience is engaged and with me, or if their attention is dwindling. If I write a book or an article, I can see the sales or circulation numbers to determine if I've reached and continue to reach my intended audience. But, on social media, the only way you know if you are hitting your target, is the response you get from friends and friends of friends. So, please, let me know your opinion; should I continue?

The last thing I want is to be the cause of any person being turned off to Christ! I know I have been the "positivity guy" for several years now, but we all have our doubts from time-to-time. It's probably just a fleeting thought that I might be wasting my time, but I honestly want to be considerate of the people I care about. When we approach a crossroad, it's important that we know where we are going. We need to check our maps to make sure we are not missing our target. My friends are my connection to my North Star. You all give meaning to the Map that will guide me for the remainder of 2023 and beyond.

So, my question for this day's devotional is: SHOULD I CONTINUE? Give me a thumbs up if you think I should continue!

My Prayer: Dear Lord, my Savior God, and Foundational Rock of my life, I pray that the Meditations of my mind, the words I write, the heartfelt emotions I stir, the LOVE I offer, and the guidance for Faith in You and The Christ Jesus I provide, are pleasing to you and not just one more "resounding gong or clanging cymbal!" I so want to always be true to 1 Corinthians 13: 13 "And now these three remain: faith, hope and love. But the greatest of these is love." Also, help me be fully aware of your presence in my life, in my surroundings, and others. I can be too quick to draw conclusions, which in all honesty is being judgmental. Forgive my impertinence and failures, and help me always see the Good in others, even those who I've chosen to exclude from my daily experience. Open my Heart! Open my Mind! Open my Soul! Open my Eyes, Ears, and every other Sensory Ability so that I might fully engage all my abilities in your Creation and enjoy it in its fullest splendor. It is abundant and Beautiful. All Gratitude belongs to you. AMEN

Kay Decker's Comment was: Yes, please do. Some days it is like you know just what path I am walking on that day and say just what I need to hear. And you know the sandboxes I play in, I need all the good word I can get. Thank you so much for doing what you do.

Julie Johnson's comment: It is not how many you reach, but you reach one person who may be truly in need of your thoughts.

Tom Butler writes: You have quite a bit of competition in my feed on this Jay. A few years a go I realized that the only people I talked to one day were current or retired pastors. It seems that everything I am involved with lately, outside my job in my passion for local government and community building is filled with religious leaders of all sorts. And you and they have really had an influence on me.

Carolyn Schumacher's comment: I look forward to your posts, Jay. Thank you for Your time.

Dr. Lowell Walsworth's comment: Please continue.

Robin Schuler writes: Inspiring discipleship; Thank You.

Mary Dost's comment: Thank you for your daily inspirations.

Jackie Gilbert-Williams Comment: Please continue. I enjoy reading your posts and I find them both thought provoking and inspirational.

Day 103: A Devotional for Understanding and Acceptance

My question from yesterday was answered with a resounding round of support. Thank you, friends, for being there in my brief moment of doubt. I appreciate the comments and it reminded me why we have these groups called churches. The fellowship and support that Christian's can give one another is extraordinary.

As a young Christian, we had a group that met once a week that we referred to as our koinonia. In Acts 2:42, we are introduced to **The Fellowship of the Believers, which in Greek is called** koinonia. "They devoted themselves to the apostles' teaching and to fellowship, to the breaking of bread and to prayer." Acts 2:42 Based on the positive responses I received to my devotional post yesterday, I was reminded that the fellowship we've experienced with this series, is in the best sense of the Greek word, KOINONIA. The beauty of the fellowship of Followers of Christ is in the openness of that fellowship! All are welcome. Christ will not reject you! People may reject Christ; that is the choice we all get.

As we progress towards the day of Pentecost, the day when the Holy Spirit Came to and washed over the Apostles, we will explore the truth of this fellowship. As Christians, our job is to share the Love of Christ with all who choose to be part of our fellowship! People may reject our Love, but that does not mean we stop sharing our Love!

My Prayer: Holy Creator God, thank you for bringing the idea of Koinonia to us. The fellowship we find, as we support one another, will help us stay positive, which will be the way we continue to bring your word of salvation to all who Open their hearts, minds, and doors to all who wish to explore our Faith. Renew a loving spirit, gracious demeanor, and faithful actions in all your children. It will be Love that Heals our hurting world. Let us Love so much that hate withers like the fig tree that would not bear fruit. All of this we pray in the Name of our Lord and Savior, Jesus Christ. AMEN

Day 104: A Devotional for Understanding and Acceptance

What is the Key to happiness? I thought we might turn our attention to the concept of happiness. We have survived another winter, with the gloominess of February and March behind us, we can turn our attention to sunnier days, warmer weather, and more time enjoying your creation. Some people deal with those months better than others. And some folks suffer through them more than others. What is it about the human condition that results in these differences?

It's too easy to say that we cause these discrepancies by our mindsets but pointing that out is also counterproductive. In order for any individual to improve their lot in life, they must have the key to unlock the door that prevents them from finding Joy in Life. There are 3 parts to the key. Part 1 is the handle of the key and that represents Love we give to God. The second part of the key is the straight length that will hold the teeth that will turn in the lock and open the door. That straight length is our basis of love for one another, which is based on how we feel about ourselves. We have difficulty loving others if we do not love ourselves. Finally, part three of the key is very diverse. To open the lock, there are several separate levers within the lock that must be turned at the same time. Each of the levers is unconditional shared love. We are happiest when we share God's love with those we love, but that happiness increases when the Love we share helps those who really need a good dose of God's unconditional Love. Our happiness needs love; especially the love of those who have no requirement to Love You! So, why would Jesus waste his time loving people who have never truly loved anyone but themselves? Because He is filled with an infinite measure of holy, pure, and indescribable love. We are important to God our Holy Parent not because of what we've accomplished, but because we are all His children. "God demonstrates his own love for us in this: While we were still sinners, Christ died for us." (Romans 5:8)

We don't have to earn His love; we simply (need to) accept it. (Ephesians 2:8-9) When we feel love, it triggers the production and release of dopamine, the happiness hormone. I have personally experienced the impact my freely sharing God's Love with people who desperately needed that love. Nearly once a week, I hear from students, athletes, colleagues, friends and just everyday people I've come into contact with, who have affirmed that my commitment to share God's Love positively affected them.

My Prayer: Hear my prayer Gracious Creator God; I am full of gratitude for the very positive affect my sharing your Unconditional Love, freely given to me, with everyone I see who seems to need a good dose of that love! Help me teach the key to happiness I outlined in this devotional. Please dear Lord help others realize that by sharing hate, (no matter what experience has generated that hate,) caused emotional pain and prevents the happiness we all seek! Not just in others, but in us as well. Remind us that Happiness is not produced from things, accomplishments, activities, pleasure or power. Satisfaction resulting from those things is generally short-lived and produces an addiction-like response. We need more and more of those things to maintain a level of satisfaction that lets us feel like we are happy! Your unconditional Love is the only thing that produces real happiness, and all we need to do is accept it! And when we spread that Love, we generate happiness wherever we go! Again, we praise you and thank you for Loving us! AMEN

Day 105: A Devotional for Understanding and Acceptance

We all have those people in life that we are so close to you, that you just know if you had never met them, your life would not have been the same. Other than my immediate family, I have a few of those. My roommates in college, colleagues over the years, some fraternity brothers, teammates from my years playing baseball; these people definitely made a big difference in my life. We reach an age when many of these people are getting on in years, and begin to pass on to their next phase of the human experience. In the past 3 years, I've had a number of these key people, that have died and with each passing a little piece of me, a spark of light, is extinguished.

Most recently, a fraternity brother, Rev. Tom Christell succumbed to the effects of Alzheimer's. Tom and I road from Rock Island to Chicago on a bus a few times, on a train another time, and when I finally had a car, I would give home a ride to meet his dad at the State of Illinois Building in downtown Chicago. We had many deep discussions, which often ended in a good laugh as we realized we were taking ourselves way too seriously.

After College, we went our separate ways. Tom to the Lutheran School of Theology in Chicago, and me into the world of secondary Education. We would occasionally talk, and our wives kept in touch. Barb and Patty (known as Tizzy to us) were sorority sisters in college as well. A little over a year and a half ago, we got a phone call. Tom was trying to make sure he talked to his good friends before Alzheimer's destroyed his memory. I hadn't realized he had been diagnosed and during our conversation, he seemed like it must have been an incorrect diagnosis. But Tizzy assured us that Tom was having a really good day and that some of the medication he was taking seemed to help. I've known people who've lived for several years after an Alzheimer's diagnosis, but that didn't happen for Tom. Last September he went into a memory care facility. Neuropathy was huge problem. He lost feeling in his extremities, and finally an injury to a toe led to sepsis, kidney failure and a rather rapid descent into home hospice care and just the other day, he passed. I'm sure he was Greeted by our Savior.

The hardest part of turning that corner and heading into that HOME stretch is the simple knowledge of the people you will be missing. So many wonderful people who helped you deal with so many personal issues and tragedies, gone and so many fewer to rely on. At these difficult times it's good to know that: "The Lord is near to the brokenhearted and saves the crushed in spirit." Psalm 34:18

And in Matthew 5 verse 4 Jesus tells us: "Blessed are they that mourn: for they shall be comforted." These are comforting words, but it doesn't eliminate the hurt.

My Prayer: Dear Jesus, I know you have received Rev. Thomas B. Christell Jr. with open arms and A Gracious well done Good and Faithful Servant! I pray for Tizzy and their kids and grandkids and all those who knew and loved Tom! It is hard to lose those you love, but we can be assured this is not the end. I look forward to the day when our spirits have the opportunity to commiserate and do a lot of catching up! Thank you, dear Jesus, our hope, redemption, and comfort. In you we place our faith. AMEN

Day 106: A Devotional for Understanding and Acceptance

Russia invades The Ukraine. Mass Shootings in the US. Israel and Palestinian Muslims are still fighting. Drought, forest and brush fires, then rain, mudslides, the huge snow storms, and avalanches! Deadly hurricanes, tornadoes, arguments about denomination doctrine, not to mention the political wars between the far right and the far left; not just in the US, but around the world!

I have a neighbor that has been watching a TV Evangelist, and that evangelist has been preaching all the signs of the apocalypse are now evident! The end is near!

Let's look at all the times in human history when those who implied that they had with a pipeline of information, directly from God. They have predicted the end of life as we know it. Before we look at some of these predictors, let's take a brief look at what Jesus said!

"At that time if anyone says to you, 'Look, here is the Messiah!' or, 'Look, there he is!' do not believe it. For false messiahs and false prophets will appear and perform signs and wonders to deceive, if possible, even the elect. So be on your guard; I have told you everything ahead of time. But in those days, following that distress, the sun will be darkened, and the moon will not give its light;" Mark 13:21-24 But about that day or hour no one knows, not even the angels in heaven, nor the Son, but only the Father. Mark 13:32

•365 CE **Hilary of Poitiers** (Bishop) predicted the end time by the end of the year!

•375–400 CE Martin of Tours (Bishop) was not able to predict a specific year, but he was sure it would be in that last quarter of the 4th Century.

•27 May 482 CE Hydatius (another Bishop) narrowed down to a Day!

•500 CE no fewer than 4 religious leaders predicted it would happen that year.

•1000(a millennium) Pope Sylvester II predicted this one!

Let's jump ahead another millennium.

•2026 Messiah Foundation International

•2028 Kent Hovind an evangelist

Everyone, please pay attention to Mark 13:32! And, Follow Jesus' final commands, The Great Commission:

- Love God
- Love Each other as Christ Loved us
- Make Disciples of all people throughout the world.

If we are as busy as we can be doing these things, we won't have to worry. We will be ready! He will come like a thief in the night. We will have no warning! So, stop trying to force the event. Your power of prediction is useless. You lack the physical strength, the character, and the intuitive capacity to do anything about it, other than the Great Commission. Adhere to these commands and you will be ready.

My Prayer: We pray to you dear Gracious Creator God: help us be more like what Jesus asked us to be and less like the control freaks we quite often try to be. Although this seems very simplistic, Teach us to Let Go, and Let You! There is not a need for us to do anything other than adhere to the final commands outlined above. Nothing else matters! BY STICKING TO THE LOVE GOD, Love others, and make disciples everywhere we go! We've done what we were taught to do. AMEN

Day 107: A Devotional for Understanding and Acceptance

Over the past 4 years, so many people have undergone some major life changing operational cognitive restructuring! Operational Cognitive restructuring is a process by which our fundamental actions, thoughts and beliefs are questioned. As a result we either change what what we are doing, or we change what we are thinking either to align with our beliefs or to become a precursor for a revised set of beliefs and values. Failure to do so results in Cognitive Dissonance. The uncomfortable feeling that something is just wrong.

With Covid 19 arriving on the scene in late 2019 and very early 2020, we were faced with a chilling choice. Should we protect all people, some people, or just let the chips fall where they may? No matter what anyone in a position of any authority did, they were opening themselves up to extraordinary criticism. What was most important: Freedom, research, the economy, or people? Through this all, the biggest loser was trust. It seems like no trusts anyone any more. Now people seem to only trust people who say what is in alignment with what they think they believe. The sad thing is, the people who we seem to have 100% alignment to, have the amazing opportunity to pull the wool so far over our eyes that we may never recognize the truth again!

What can we do about that? There is only one remedy for this pernicious disease! We need a great big dose of Unconditional Love from God. This is the only medicine that can cure this pandemic of MISTRUST! This pandemic is far more deadly than was Covid. This Pandemic can kill instantly without warning. One minute you're happy and content and the next you're gone!

My Prayer: Let's all pray together that God, through Jesus our Savior, will come, once again, to our rescue. Please Holy God, give us the power of discernment so that we can tell the wolves and Jackals from the Lambs. It's it always easy because many times we've become so familiar with the Jackals that we're comfortable with them. We think they're the good guys because they've learned to say what we want to hear. But what we need to hear is the Commandments Jesus Gave us and all of these have one central focus: LOVE. Love never fails. But where there are prophecies, they will cease; where there are tongues, they will be stilled; where there is knowledge, it will pass away. For we know in part and we prophesy in part, but when completeness l, what is in part disappears. When I was a child, I talked like a child, I thought like a child, I reasoned like a child. When I became a man, I put the ways of childhood behind me. **For now we see only a reflection**

as in a mirror; then we shall see face to face. (We think we've seen the truth: Have we)* **Now I know in part; then I shall know fully, even as I am fully known.** (We think we know the truth! But DO WE?)* And now these three remain: faith, hope and love. But the greatest of these is love. 1 Corinthians 13: 8-13 *AMEN* *Parenthetic statements are my interjected questions!

Day 108: A Devotional for Understanding and Acceptance

How do we know if we've been saved? Can we ever truly know if our faith is strong enough to "Qualify" for entry into heaven? Let's see how we're doing on our faith Journey!

Jesus replied, "Truly I tell you, if you have faith and do not doubt, not only can you do what was done to the fig tree, but also you can say to this mountain, 'Go, throw yourself into the sea,' and it will be done. Matthew 21:21 Anyone cause a Fig Tree to wither? How about moving a mountain? No, why not? Oh, your faith is too weak.

Shortly before dawn Jesus went out to them, walking on the lake. When the disciples saw him walking on the lake, they were terrified. "It's a ghost," they said, and cried out in fear. But Jesus immediately said to them: "Take courage! It is I. Don't be afraid."

"Lord, if it's you," Peter replied, "tell me to come to you on the water." "Come," he said.

Then Peter got down out of the boat, walked on the water and came toward Jesus. But when he saw the wind, he was afraid and, beginning to sink, cried out, "Lord, save me!"

Immediately Jesus reached out his hand and caught him. "You of little faith," he said, "why did you doubt?"

And when they climbed into the boat, the wind died down. Then those who were in the boat worshiped him, saying, "Truly you are the Son of God."

Matthew 14:25-33 Anyone walk on water recently? How about turn water into wine? Restore sight to the blind? Restore hearing to the deaf? Instantaneously heal sicknesses, or raise the dead? Neither did I.

Maybe Jesus knew it would be easier for us to put our faith in humans than in God. Perhaps that's why he commanded us to Love! We can all Love, can't we? He did not command us to correct the behaviors of others, and severely punish those who won't obey. Nor did he command that we build personal wealth or go to war with those who have wronged us. If God had wanted us to do that, John 3:16 would read:

For God so Wanted to Control the Actions and Behavior of humans that he gave his one and only Son, to get them all to toe the LINE! But that's not what John 3:16 says, is it? We all know it says:

For God so **loved** the world that he gave his one and only Son, that whoever believes in him shall not perish but have eternal life.

My Prayer: Gracious God, our faith is weak, please help strengthen it. We will know our faith is strong when the Greatest Commandments become more important than everything else. More important than rules, order, structure, or freedom. Freedom without Love is useless. Structure without Love is hollow. Order without Love is a line leading nowhere. Rules without Love is tyranny. Help us to recognize and know your love so fully and intimately that all else pales in comparison. And The World will know we are Christians by our Love! **AMEN HALLELUJAH AMEN**

Day 109: A Devotional for Understanding and Acceptance

How long is a day when the sun has not yet been formed? Recent photographs from the new Webb Telescope out in deep space, show spectacular views of how our Universe is still in a state of continuous change.

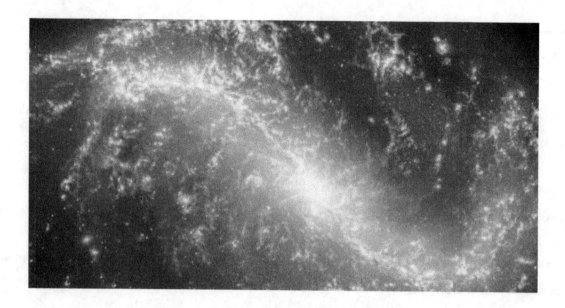

The picture shows new solar systems that were formed millions of years ago; however, they are not static. They continue to change. How old is our Universe? Was our planet formed 6,000 years ago or 6 million years ago or 6 billion years ago? That question misses the point! A much better question is How long is a year in God's Measuring System. "But do not overlook this one fact, beloved, that with the Lord one day is as a thousand years, and a thousand years as one day."(2Peter 3:8)

We measure our days as being 24 hours long, but we have decided that the length of a day is based on one revolution of the Earth on its Axis. Once again, we try to fit God into a box that is defined totally in human terms. Isn't it completely possible that 6 billion human years is but 6,000 Years in God's way of viewing the creation process. And how does this creation happen? That is a matter of quantum mechanics. God has left hints through our history and scientists have slowly uncovered those hints. The more we learn from science, the more we begin to understand the nature of God, and how everything was created.

How long does the creation process takes, and when it began is not the question we should be asking? The question that needs to be asked is Why has creation happened at all? What is the purpose underlying the existence of anything and everything? Are we all just an accident of the universe? Intuitively, we all sense a connection to other people. What is it that draws us to some and seems to separate us from others? The more we investigate our universe the more questions we generate.

Of all the places in the Bible to learn the lessons of the nature of creation, the one that has surprised me most is Job 12:7-12. We often only think of the suffering of Job, but in these verses, we see the true Glory of God!

7 "But ask the animals, and they will teach you, or the birds in the sky, and they will tell you;

8 or speak to the earth, and it will teach you, or let the fish in the sea inform you.

9 Which of all these does not know that the hand of the LORD has done this?

10 In his hand is the life of every creature and the breath of all mankind.

11 Let the heavens rejoice, let the earth be glad; let the sea resound, and all that is in it.

12 Let the fields be jubilant, and everything in them; let all the trees of the forest sing for joy.

My Prayer: Heavenly Gracious God, you have provided us with an amazing creation that we are responsible for. Help us be considerate of all species and all the essential materials needed for our continued existence. Many of us have come to the conclusion that it doesn't matter who has caused any of the major problems we face, man or nature or sunspots; if we are to continue as the glorious creation of God, we are tasked with using God's Creation with all the reverence, care, and love due to such a magnificent and Majestic Creator! The day of my personal birth is not significant, nor is the number of years, months, days, hours, and minutes I've been alive. What matters is that God has loved each of us unconditionally. That unconditional Love is a Love that is given whether or not it is acknowledged, reciprocated, and even if the other individual despises the one expressing that unconditional love. Difficult for humans but so easy for a loving God. We praise you and thank you for even having this opportunity to exist at all. AMEN

Day 110: A Devotional for Understanding and Acceptance

Why does our world keep heading down wrong paths and keep causing pain and suffering? Too many times the actions that cause this suffering is generated from incredible fear. Too many people have been scared into doing that which we find reprehensible by people who are very misguided in their beliefs. When a few people of influence who have trusted the wrong source for what is real and trustworthy, start shouting there's a real threat over there! Everyone immediately assumes their political posture and either starts falling in line with the wrongheadedness or they jump to the defense of the individuals or groups that the "threatened" people are riled up about. And as you read this, you are probably thinking the wrongheaded people are those that think differently than you! I'm saying, it doesn't make any difference! From time to time, we're all wrongheaded about things.

So, what's the solution. There's a simple solution but it requires great cooperation, patience, and dedication on the part of everyone. The simple solution is to look for the JOY, in everyone, everywhere, in every single solitary thing, and every time we start to **REACT**! Barb (my wife) and I looked at a photograph of us, together, pre-Covid, with our little vineyard in the background. We were so full of happiness and joy. Today we said, how do we get back to that wonderful state of Joy. The current state dis-ease is pernicious. It creeps in and sets up its nasty little camp without us even realizing it. Then we're hooked! It's like an addiction. The only way to overcome addiction is to make sure you don't give in to temptation.

Read these words from Jesus:

Matthew 6:19-34

"Do not store up for yourselves treasures on earth, where moths and vermin destroy, and where thieves break in and steal. But store up for yourselves treasures in heaven, (how? Love God and Love others)* where moths and vermin do not destroy, and where thieves do not break in and steal. For where your treasure is, there your heart will be also. (I believe everything else hinges on this. Failure here haunts us all)*

"The eye is the lamp of the body. If your eyes are healthy, (by healthy, Jesus is telling us to focus on Loving God and one another)* your whole body will be full of light. But if your eyes are unhealthy, (focused on your treasures)* your whole body will be full of darkness. If then the light within you is darkness, how great is that darkness!

"No one can serve two masters. Either you will hate the one and love the other, or you will be devoted to the one and despise the other. You cannot serve both God and money. (treasures)*

"Therefore, I tell you, do not worry about your life, what you will eat or drink; or about your body, what you will wear. Is not life more than food, and the body more than clothes? Look at the birds of the air; they do not sow or reap or store away in barns, and yet your heavenly Father feeds them. Are you not much more valuable than they? Can any one of you by worrying add a single hour to your life?

"And why do you worry about clothes? See how the flowers of the field grow. They do not labor or spin. Yet I tell you that not even Solomon in all his splendor was dressed like one of these. If that is how God clothes the grass of the field, which is here today and tomorrow is thrown into the fire, will he not much more clothe you—you of little faith? So do not worry, saying, 'What shall we eat?' or 'What shall we drink?' or 'What shall we wear?' For the unbelievers run after all these things, and your heavenly Father knows that you need them. But seek first his kingdom and his righteousness, and all these things will be given to you as well. Therefore do not worry about tomorrow, for tomorrow will worry about itself. Each day has enough trouble of its own.

*My clarification of how these trip us up!

We truly need to become fully aware of how what we are doing, on a daily, even on a minute-by-minute basis, continuously puts us in opposition to the Peace, Love, and Joy God wants for everyone, every single human being. If you store up treasures, you don't trust God! If you worry about what you will eat, drink, or wear, you don't trust God!

My prayer today is short and simple: Dear Jesus, please help us trust God as much as YOU did. Help us serve our God and Savior, not Wealth and Treasure! Help to trust God for all our needs and help us to always, as you did, care for others by being the hands, feet, voice, and heart of God to those who need it. We ask this in the Your Name, Lord Jesus! AMEN

Day 111: A Devotional for Understanding and Acceptance

Until Pentecost, I will be sharing some suggestions on how we can become more aware of how our thinking and the actions those thoughts generate affect our state of mind. Today, I'm going to introduce a focusing activity, that I call taking off your "Sleep" mask. If there's too much activity going on around you when you are trying to go to sleep, you can put on a sleep mask, which blocks out light and helps us get to sleep. Imagine if you forgot to remove the sleep mask in the morning and you thought all the light in the world had gone out. And no one could convince you that all you had to do is remove your mask and you could see clearly! Sounds ridiculous: But?

Suppose a person stated a fact that opposed a political view you held onto with every fiber of your being! How would you react? Over the past 20 years or so, I'm pretty sure you would not listen to that person. In fact, Americans have become very adept at calling people who have ideas that are counter to their way of thinking, either Fascists or Socialists, depending on which end of the spectrum they are looking from. The exercise I call **Taking Off Your Sleep Mask,** is a simple act of pausing and considering the other person's point-of-view. I know that would be very difficult for some people. I have a conservative friend who often likes to say to his liberal friends that he could agree with them but then we'd all be wrong.

As a Christian, however, I suggest that as each person in a disagreement state their point of view, and then answer the following questions:

- How would following your ideas affect people with differing opinions?
- How does your opinion align with what Christ Commands us to do?
- How will changing your opinion affect you personally? Today, in a week, in a month, in a year?

Our political environment is not about doing what we think is best, it's about making sure the opposition does not succeed. As those efforts drag us all into a very bad state, everyone loses. I suggest we all practice taking off our sleep masks and look for ways we can work together. And let's stop stirring the pot and demand those that represent us at the local, county, state, and federal levels do the same!

"Above all, love each other deeply because love covers over a multitude of sins. Offer hospitality to one another without grumbling. Each of you should use whatever gift you have received to serve others, as faithful stewards of God's grace in its various forms." 1 Peter 4:8-10

"And let us consider how we may spur one another on toward love and good deeds, not giving up meeting together, as some are in the habit of doing, but encouraging one another…." Hebrews 10:24,25

Both Peter and Paul truly understood how important working together is. If our differences keep us from finding ways to work together, we will ultimately fail.

My Prayer: Gracious Creator God, help us get along with one another. We can each easily see that there are people who see the world differently than us. Remind us to take our sleep masks off and truly seek to understand before we push others to try to understand us. My way or the highway has never been a good leadership philosophy. Help us to seek cooperation and collaboration with those who have differing opinions. Help us to always look at our Christian responsibility as being, how we can share our efforts and love to make disciples of the world! Will what I think "we should do" help or hurt our chances of making disciples throughout the world. AMEN

Day 112: A Devotional for Understanding and Acceptance

Why won't anybody listen to me? I wish I had a dollar for every time I've heard people ask this question? It's a pandemic in its own right. Everyone's talking and no one's listening.

If you want to really know what the state of our world really is at any given time, just carefully listen to as many people as you possibly can without interrupting or even making a comment unless they ask for your thoughts. Everyone is right. No one's listening, including them. And even if you find the rare person who's listening, they are probably listening through their own filters. As a result, they may miss what you are saying because they only hear things through a "what-they-want-to-hear" filtering systems.

What can we learn from the Bible about the need to listen to rather than always being the one who is trying to get your voice heard?

Know this, my beloved brothers: let every person be quick to hear, slow to speak, slow to anger; James 1:19 A fool takes no pleasure in understanding, but only in expressing his opinion. Proverbs 18:2 So faith comes from hearing, and hearing through the word of Christ. Romans 10:17. If anyone thinks he is religious and does not bridle his tongue but deceives his heart, this person's religion is worthless. James 1:26 And he said to them, "Pay attention to what you hear: with the measure you use, it will be measured to you, and still more will be added to you. Mark 4:24

My Prayer: Dear Savior Jesus, we ask you to help us all become better listeners. We ask that our wisdom be seasoned with the Love You so graciously heaped upon us. Help us get beyond ourselves and truly listen to the cry of the people. Our Leaders, both Conservative and Liberal have made a habit of only listening enough to know how to scare us into believing they can save us from "the OTHERS!" We know that our salvation can only come from you. We do not need to be saved from others; it is our own selfish motives that creates the possibility of eternal separation from God. The Greatest Sin of All is Not Loving God with our who hearts, minds, efforts, soul, and in everything we do! We take short cuts. We think we can be good enough; but we only gain strength through Loving God and Every Single Human we come into contact with. Hate is what allows us to turn our backs on those who've fallen on hard times, are born without hope into poverty, or those who look, speak, or have cultures that are different. Forgive us Lord and help us remove the Planks from our own Eyes and then we can help our neighbors with the specks in their eyes. AMEN

Day 113: A Devotional for Understanding and Acceptance

Do some people just have it really easy? Or have we just misread how hard they've had to work! We often ignore how hard people work during their planning, practice, and personal performance review and performance adjustment process to make their success seem like it was effortless. Those who don't take that approach to performance improvement miss the mark. They attribute success to luck or a special gift of talent that is so rare. But research done by numerous talent experts tells us that innate talent is often a curse for many.

The highly talented, at an early age, can do things other kids their age have difficulty matching. They often coast through times while less talented kids, who in their early years struggle to do as well, must develop intense practice procedures and a work ethic that will keep them in the mix. Eventually, all that hard work will pay huge dividends for those willing to invest their time, energy, and effort. So, we end up with 4 tiers of performance. The lowest tier has people who were short on talent in their developmental years and also lacked to support and grit to put in the time, energy, and effort to truly improve. Next, we have the talented people who coasted and never worked hard enough to allow their gift to grow and develop. The third level up are those people who may not have had the massive talent as a young person but worked extremely hard and made the most of the talent they had. And the top level are the people who took every bit of talent they'd been given and worked extremely hard to develop that talent and continuously look for ways to improve it even more!

Many people think swimmers like Michael Phelps and Katie Ledecky, Basketball players like Michael Jordan and Candace Parker, and Sprinters like Usain Bolt and Florence Griffith-Joyner, to mention only a few extraordinary athletes, never had to work very hard. They all achieved elite status by applying extraordinary training programs to the talents they possessed. It is the diligent attention to detail, hard work, along with a focus on the talents they possessed, that helped these athletes achieve along with grit, tenacity, and persistence. These are all Biblically Supported behaviors.

Dr. Angela Duckworth defines Grit as: The relentless resolve to keep pursuing a desired goal and not giving up. Wouldn't you know? Your grandfather was right after all: Success does look a lot like hard work. These Biblical Figures definitely showed grit! Abraham and Sarah, Noah, Jacob,

Joseph, both Peter and Paul. Luke 18:1-8, tells a parable of a widow who keeps coming back to receive justice from a Judge who didn't want to side with her, but finally gives in and States: "I will give her justice, so that she will not beat me down by her continual coming"(back to argue her case!) "If we endure, we will also reign with Him. If we deny Him, He also will deny us." 2 Timothy 2:12. This is a pretty reasonable description of Being Spiritually Tenacious.

My Prayer: Gracious God, you've given each of us talents. Help us develop and hone these talents so that we might more effectively serve you. Help us have the grit needed to put in the work that will lead to us becoming the best possible Servant we can be. Help us to practice our faith with the persistence that demonstrates our desire for your Love and demonstrates our undying love for You. And dear Jesus, help us be persistent in our prayers so that we can bring Christ's message to every corner of this world: Love God, Love Each Other, and Make Disciples in Every region and Nation in the world! AMEN

Day 114: A Devotional for Understanding and Acceptance

What is the product of Love? Love Creates Loyalty!

What is the product of hate? Hate creates distrust and deceit! The ancient world was much different than today. Societal roles depended upon one's ability to do certain tasks. But there were 2 things that we totally independent of one's own ability, Love and hate. Whether or not you shared love was a matter of personal will, and that does not require any unusual ability. You simply have to choose to Love! The same goes for hate; it's a matter of personal choice. I choose Love! What will you choose? We know what choice our Lord Jesus Made. The scriptures are clear!

"But I say to you who hear, love your enemies, do good to those who hate you," Luke 6:27

"Anyone who does not love does not know God, because God is love." 1 John 4:8 "If you love me, you will keep my commandments." John 14:15

And he said to him, "You shall love the Lord your God with all your heart and with all your soul and with all your mind. This is the greatest and first commandment. And a second is like it: You shall love your neighbor as yourself. On these two commandments depend all the Law and the Prophets." Matthew 22:37-40

My Prayer: Jesus, our Hope, Redeemer, and Savior of all who are aware and choose to follow! Forgive us for our failure to remove all hate from our lives and more importantly, forgive us for our failure to Love one another as you have commanded us to! We show our contempt for these crucial Commandments when we believe it is ok to hate! I ask dear Jesus, that you would touch as many people as possible and ask them to make a commitment to Love! Please ask every person who sees this devotional to declare "I choose LOVE!" I will be first and add my declaration as the very first comment! AMEN

Day 115: A Devotional for Understanding and Acceptance

"Ask and it will be given to you; seek and you will find; knock and the door will be opened to you. For everyone who asks receives; the one who seeks finds; and to the one who knocks, the door will be opened." Matthew 7:7,8

Why would Jesus say this? We all know we keep seeking yet never find it. I ask, yet I don't see that I've received what I asked for. Finally, maybe I've been knocking at the wrong door!

Wait a minute, what's this I'm reading just a few lines down?

"Not everyone who says to me, 'Lord, Lord,' will enter the kingdom of heaven, but only the one who does the will of my Father who is in heaven." Matthew 7: 21

What is the Will of the Father? I am to Love God more than anything else? And I am to Love my fellow human beings as Christ has Loved ME! The verdict: GUILTY on Both Charges. I admit, there are times when I just don't Love God as much as I've been commanded to love him! How do I know? Because I've failed the second part. There are plenty of people who just seem to make a sane, reasonably faithful Christian hope they are be-felled with a biblical malady. However, I know I'm no prize but God Loves me so much more than I deserve! Jesus is asking us to Love others as he has Loved Us!

Let's get back to Matthew 7:7,8. If it seems like we aren't receiving, finding, and having doors flung wide open for us; I think we know why! Love is the only answer. No other action will do! We need to get that huge "I" beam out of our eyes before we start requiring others to remove the tiny speck from their own eye. The huge "I" Beam, is our Ego! The tiny little being that has a tendency to lock love out because we don't agree, can't see ourselves doing that, don't care for, can't understand, etc., etc., etc.!

My Prayer: Gracious God, let me find my way to LOVE! I realize that my lack of unconditional love for others is holding me back. My inability to put aside my prejudice, bias, and demands of others creates a stumbling block like no other. And I know we all do it! Forgive my shortcomings and help me LOVE! I know LOVE is the answer! I do trust and I am Loyal. Please help me extinguish each flicker of doubt and each blip of disloyalty. I shall not expect anything and will be grateful for everything. You are my rock and fortress. I you everything is possible. AMEN.

Day 116: A Devotional for Understanding and Acceptance

How do we show love to others when we all seem to be so angry? And Why's everyone so angry? It's a common feeling these days and my opinion is that everyone feels short-changed. Somebody else is getting the stuff we've wanted, and they didn't earn it and that makes me MAD! And when I'm MAD, I'm usually Sad and it's hard to be glad when you're so used to being Mad and Sad.

So how do we get to GLAD, when we're so tied up in MAD-SAD knot! The key is in counting our blessings. Stop focusing on what's wrong because we always move towards our focus. To move in a different direction, we must focus on the target that is definitely a better place than where we are now. Our distress results from thinking about what we do not have. Satisfaction results from knowing what do have and then being grateful for being so blessed! When you count your blessings, what you are doing is acknowledging all the good in your life. If you can't think of anything good in your life, I ask a simple question, are you the most devastated, unhealthy, unattractive, unloved, uneducated, untalented person in the world? If you are, you are one of a kind, and being such a person is so unique, I bet there are people who would pay you to tell your story which would require a great deal of research! It is the art of turning lemons into lemonade!

Do You feel unworthy? Let's see what Jesus says about how many times we should forgive, which then says how many times we will be forgiven.

Matthew 18: 21-22: Then Peter came to Jesus and asked, "Lord, how many times shall I forgive my brother or sister who sins against me? Up to seven times?" Jesus answered, "I tell you, not seven times, but seventy-times-seven!" By my calculation that's 490 times! How on Earth are we supposed to do that? It is a state of being! Jesus understood that we let our thinking over-shadow our spirit. For some reason, we think that logic is more powerful than the spirit. Jesus also knew that this was not true. Logic is like iron! And like iron it is unbending to most other matter. The Spirit is like a Laser beam that cuts through an iron barrier like a hot knife through butter. The most powerful spirit in the universe is the spirit of our Living God. Jesus also knows that there is a piece of This Spirit in all of us. This is what separates Living from on-Living entities. To find your inner spirit, sit quietly and just focus on your own breath. As you inhale silently say YAH and as you exhale silently say WEH!

My Prayer: Lord Jesus, teach us how to connect with Our Amazing Creator God. You've given us a prayer, and most of us use that prayer regularly, but we don't always know how to put our insecurities aside and ask with a pure heart. Teach us to always ask out of love and seek with a loving heart! Help us to desire to knock on doors that not only benefit us but are a significant help to others. We realize that we are at our best when we act out of love. Help us examine our every motive and root out the motivations that exclude, belittle and diminish others. Since you and your heavenly Parent Creator God, are the very definition of the Power of Love, let us demonstrate our Love through our humble connection to your uplifting spirit: Today, Tomorrow, and Forever! AMEN

Day 117: A Devotional for Understanding and Acceptance

What is our soul? The soul is the spiritual part of a human being which is <u>immortal</u>. It is our soul that possesses the potential for connecting to the Spirit of the Living God. Every person has that possibility for connecting with that Spirit and Jesus gave us the formula for activating that connection. The formula is two parts unconditional Love. One given to God through the only child of the living God to Physically Overcome Death, Christ Jesus. The second part is to be given unconditionally to every human we interact with. This Love is truly amazing, the more we share, the more we have! The less we share of this love, the less we have.

Knowing that the more we share, the more we have; it becomes very difficult to understand why anyone would withhold that love from any person. But it happens. Why is that? The answer is clear, we have been programmed through years of false teaching. The false teaching is that there is a requirement for receiving love; the Love of God, the Love of your mother, the Love of your Father, the Love of teachers, the Love of your spouse, the Love of your children, and so on, and so one! Each of these are false concepts. **God does not require anything** from you for you to receive the Love that God has for you. So why do we attach conditions to the Love we share? Is it that we're afraid we will run out of Love? Is it that we are afraid of being taken advantage of? Is it because "we just don't know how?" It doesn't matter. Each of us must understand, that if you say you Love God, but have a neighbor you despise, then you cannot truly Love God; for God Loves that neighbor, and how can we Love God and despise someone that God cares so deeply about.

So how do we get there? Follow Jesus! Jesus told Peter, Immediately Jesus reached out his hand and caught him. "You of little faith," he said, "why did you doubt?" Matthew 14:31. To be able to Love people who, to you are so unlovable, you must not doubt Jesus. He said, "have faith," and "love your enemies and pray for those who persecute you." (Matthew 5:44). If you find this difficult, start off slow, spend time each day thinking positively about things that bring you joy. Every time you start thinking badly about any person, or anything else in the world, go back in your brain to that joyful experience! Try this prayer:

My Prayer: Gracious God, you have been so extraordinarily good to me. I have been blessed far more than I can imagine. You are indeed an Awesome God. Help me put the sorrow, sadness, greed and anger behind me. Touch my heart and soul so that my most common feelings are Joy, happiness, contentment, and acceptance of others that can lead, not only me, but those who I connect with to that Peace that comes from our Focused and Loving Souls! For Your Way is the Way I Choose! Being in Love with that Amazing Connection between You, my Savior God, and all of Humanity. AMEN-Hallelujah-AMEN!

Day 118: A Devotional for Understanding and Acceptance

How can I turn my life around and start seeing the beauty there is, rather than the pain and suffering I see on the News every night! "But I tell you, in this you are not right, for God is greater than any mortal. Why do you complain to him that he responds to no one's words? For God does speak—now one way, now another—though no one perceives it. In a dream, a vision of the night, when sound sleep falls on men, while they slumber in their beds, Then He opens the ears of men, and seals their instruction, That He may turn man aside from his conduct, And keep man from pride; He keeps back his soul from the pit!" Job,33:12-18

Heed this warning from the Book of Job. What you say to yourself before you fall asleep at night can be sealed in your heart and disrupt the beautiful message God has for you. Rather than all the good he wants for you, if your last thoughts, while you fall off to sleep at night, are about the bad in the world, thoughts of how you failed today, why you are so unhealthy; these will be the beliefs you have about what's going on in your world! You won't hear what God is telling you. If, as you lay down to sleep, you start counting your blessings; if you say I am so blessed, I have great health, I have all I need and more, I have wonderful relationships, I can do anything through my Lord and Savior Jesus. These thoughts will put you in good stead for the coming day. Try this for 40 days.

There is amazing research being done regarding people who give thanks to the Lord for blessing them so abundantly and how that makes such a positive impact in their lives. We can change the world through the abundant Love of God. But it will take more than 100 people to do so. It will take millions of people becoming true Disciples of Christ. But the 100 people who have liked and made positive comments about this Devotional if each of those would invite 10 people. Imagine how the message will spread. Think about it, I have. I have thought of an entire process that just keeps growing. Humanity, in my Book, is worth it!

My Prayer: Gracious God, thank you for saving my soul! I pray that we will save many more through your amazing and abundant Love! Give us the direction and will to follow it with intensity and purpose. I am grateful for my health, the energy I have to face each day, we have all we need and then some, and each night as I lay down to sleep, I am assured of my salvation through my savior Christ Jesus. AMEN

Day 119: A Devotional for Understanding and Acceptance

Sometimes our work is done for us by others. it is up to us to recognize that someone dear to use has done the work for us, even if that was not their intention. Thank you my dear Cousin "Pete" Shobe for making this request at this moment in time. Please read and support her in this endeavor.

In respect to the spirit of revival that is taking place around the world, I humbly ask if everyone on my timeline who believes in the power of prayer would stop what you're doing, just take a minute, and post this... I know all won't, but I hope some will.

II Chronicles 7:14 Lord, we need you !!!!!! Please sweep across this nation and heal this land. Restore our strength, renew our minds, and banish everything that is not of You. In Jesus name we pray. Amen!! Amen again I say Hallelujah Amen!

My Prayer: Thank you, Dear Jesus! You know exactly when we find ourselves in need of help from others. As we face these troubling times, we know your teachings are crystal clear. Love God and Love one another. How do we demonstrate this Love? By lifting one another up when they need it most and by always being there to answer questions when the need arises. How will we know what the best answer is for the questions posed? If we will just listen as we go to sleep each night, the answers will be there! God never fails as long as we are willing to listen. Amen!

Day 120: A Devotional for Understanding and Acceptance

Are you remembering to count your blessings each night? I know I am. I have been taking an inventory each night as I lay down to sleep. And I do very strongly believe it is paying off!

For the last several nights I have been reminding myself of how God has Blessed Me! I continue to be an extremely healthy person. We all have our moments but mine have been few, and I seem to usually recover quickly.

Also, even though as very young children, we were not very well off: 4 kids in one bedroom and a family of 6 with one bathroom? It wasn't always easy, but we never complained much. I know now that financial wellbeing has more to do with keeping your wants separate from your needs and not confusing those two. Today, I have that attitude and I believe that wealth is more about realizing that we live in an abundant world with more than enough for everyone. It's finding contentment and accepting others for their gifts that has been the real blessing for me.

In this world of influencers, I can honestly say, I've been blessed to have had some influence on a few people in my life. Unlike many of the influencers we are confronted with today, I'm not involved with influencing people to make purchases or change their style. My influence has been more about how people commit to living in this world and who they should truly trust and how we treat one another that creates satisfaction and Joy.

My fourth blessing is Joy. I have an amazing wife, 3 wonderful children and their families, and 7 grandchildren who totally understand that my message to them is: Always Remember, PAPA LOVES YOU!

"Woe to you, scribes and Pharisees, hypocrites! For you tithe mint and dill and cumin and have neglected the weightier matters of the law: justice and mercy and faithfulness. These you ought to have done, without neglecting the others." Matthew 23:23

My Prayer: Gracious Lord, we are truly grateful for our lives. We know that we have many choices to make. Some of these lead us to become less than we can be and often those choices are the easiest to make. Help us understand that without a loving commitment to You and to our fellow humans, our lives are meaningless. Without You our existence lacks purpose. Without Your Love:

If I speak in the tongues of men or of angels, but do not have love, I am only a resounding gong or a clanging cymbal. 1 Corinthians 13:1. Amen

Day 121: A Devotional for Understanding and Acceptance

When I was a child, I talked like a child, I thought like a child, I reasoned like a child. When I became a man, I set aside childish ways. Now we see but a dim reflection as in a mirror; then we shall see face to face. Now I know in part; then I shall know fully, even as I am fully known.

For children, the world is so easy to understand! There's mine and yours and if we share that's marvelous. As we grow and mature, we put away our childish ways. We discover that the world is far more complex. Some people get confused, and things get murky. Nothing seems to mean what we think they should mean. As an adult, we think we know what's right and what's wrong, but we often see our view as being what God really wants. But the time is near, when we will see things as God sees them, and we will know how far we strayed.

Paul thought he knew. He persecuted those who strayed from Jewish law and certainly these followers of Jesus were the worst kind of blasphemers. Then he literally saw the light that temporarily blinded him and when he regained his vision, he saw how far from the truth he had strayed. The last verse of 1 Corinthians 13 says: "And now these three remain: faith, hope, and love; but the greatest of these is love." That was what he had missed. The Law applied out of anger, discomfort, or hate creates horrible distortions of what God really wants. Peace, Love, and Living by Faith.

My Prayer: Holy Lord God, Jesus our Redeemer, and the universal Holy Spirit, together you create a layer of protection for our Souls. The power of this Trinity is greater and possesses more energy than any mortal human can conceive of. We thank you and ask for your forgiveness. Lead us towards a better world for all of us! We pray this in full acceptance that You can forgive what we think is so horrible, we cannot even begin to imagine why you just don't bring down punishment on this awful world. But, as always, Your vision is so much better than ours. And with that in mind, we say Again: AMEN

Day 122: A Devotional for Understanding and Acceptance

Contrast is an interesting idea. Without contrast, everything is identical. If everything is exactly the same, life as we know it would be impossible. However, when we observe contrasts between people, we run the risk of discriminating against people for trivial reasons. Race, skin color, cultural status, financial station, level of education, and religious or philosophical tradition are irrelevant in the eyes of God. All are equal!

It is what we do with the gifts we are given that God wants to see. We all can each do more than we might think. Too many do way too little. To those who have been given much, much will be expected. But it will be easier for those who have much to give much. But we rarely see that. Jesus noted that in his parable of the widow's mite.

Jesus sat down opposite the place where the offerings were put and watched the crowd putting their money into the temple treasury. Many rich people threw in large amounts. But a poor widow came and put in two very small copper coins, worth only a few cents. Calling his disciples to him, Jesus said, "Truly I tell you; this poor widow has put more into the treasury than all the others. They all gave out of their wealth; but she, out of her poverty, put in everything—all she had to live on." Mark 12: 41-44

My Prayer: Gracious God, your creation is amazingly diverse. Please Do not let us allow appearances to affect our ability to care for people. I've watched my family welcome many people into their circles that are easily rejected by most in our society. Many do not speak the same language as us. Others have a complexion that is quite different. Some have differing philosophies or religious beliefs. And we are saddened when they are abused or thought of as being somehow less than us. We all pray that we will judge people by "the content of their character and not by the color of their skin or some other physical difference that exists. We pray for a more accepting, affirming, and loving world today, tomorrow, and forever and ever, AMEN!

Day 123: A Devotional for Understanding and Acceptance

As we interact with the world, how do we change the world without the world changing us for the worse? To begin with, we need to realize that change begins with us. We must live the life that exemplifies the changes we want to see. We absolutely must understand that unless we change, nothing else will change! Too often, we want everyone else to change and we, ourselves, are flawed in another area.

With his mouth the godless man destroys his neighbor, but through knowledge the righteous will be delivered. Proverbs 11:9

For as he thinks within himself, so he is. He says to you, "Eat and drink!" But his heart is not with you. Proverbs 23:7

And He said to them, "Rightly did Isaiah prophesy of you hypocrites, as it is written: 'These people honor Me with their lips, but their heart is far away from Me'." Mark 7:6

And in the morning, 'There will be a storm today, for the sky is red and threatening.' Do you know how to discern the appearance of the sky, but cannot discern the signs of the times? Matthew 16:3

If we try to correct others, while we are still grossly flawed, we run the risk of separating ourselves from Christ. Be very weary of the temptation to call out the sins of others. You may feel their sins are horrible, but it is not ours to determine who has committed the worst sin. Do not run the risk of across did the men who called out the adulterous woman.

The teachers of the law and the Pharisees brought in a woman caught in adultery. They made her stand before the group and said to Jesus, "Teacher, this woman was caught in the act of adultery. In the Law Moses commanded us to stone such women. Now what do you say?" They were using this question as a trap, in order to have a basis for accusing him.

But Jesus bent down and started to write on the ground with his finger. When they kept on questioning him, he straightened up and said to them, "Let any one of you who is without sin be the first to throw a stone at her." Again, he stooped down and wrote on the ground. At this, those who heard began to go away one at a time, the older ones first, until only Jesus was left, with the woman still standing there. Jesus straightened up and asked her, "Woman, where are they? Has no one condemned you?" "No one, sir," she said. "Then neither do I condemn you, "Jesus declared. "Go now and leave your life of sin." John 8: 3-11

My Prayer: Gracious Creator God, you sent your Holy Child, Jesus, to us and he would not condemn this woman who had committed adultery. Let us take our marching orders from Jesus. We call ourselves Christians but choose not to follow his teaching. By so doing, we separate ourselves from God! Have Mercy on us dear Jesus. Forgive our Sins and Save our Souls! AMEN

Day 124: A Devotional for Understanding and Acceptance

How aware are you of where your mind is going on a minute-by-minute basis? If you are anything like me, your brain will take off and be traveling down some self-destructive rabbit hole and dwell there for far too long before you realize where your brain is. Once you've spent too much time there, so has your heart and spirit!

How do we pull ourselves out of these terrible places in time to salvage our hearts, souls, and connection to God? I didn't always know! But I've learned a simple solution. Whenever I begin to question, where I am? How I got here? Does anybody care? Or any similar such question! My answer is always Jesus knows! Let's look for some comfort there! Here are some passages I've found great comfort in.

May the God of hope fill you with all joy and peace as you trust in him, so that you may overflow with hope by the power of the Holy Spirit. Romans 15:13

Praise be to the God and Father of our Lord Jesus Christ, the Father of compassion and the God of all comfort, who comforts us in all our troubles, so that we can comfort those in any trouble with the comfort we ourselves receive from God. 2 Corinthians 1:3-4

"Come to me, all you who are weary and burdened, and I will give you rest. Take my yoke upon you and learn from me, for I am gentle and humble in heart, and you will find rest for your souls. For my yoke is easy and my burden is light." Matthew 11: 28-30

My Prayer: Precious Jesus, my Savior and comforter in times of distress, I am grateful for the help you give when all feels lost. As we continue to move through this life remind us, whenever we doubt, why each of us is of such great value to you. When we are reminded that your sacrifice was very personal for each of us, we are also reminded that YOU have actively reached out to every one of us, not just collective masses, but each of us; personally, and individually. That is why your touch upon my heart (yes, each person should say a very big **MY** in that spot) can bring me out of the deepest holes and raise me to the heights above all fear and trepidation. Thank you, gracious Lord! AMEN

Day 125: A Devotional for Understanding and Acceptance

What does God want from us? I know we're supposed to Love God with the Entirety of our whole BEING, but how on God's Great Creation, are we supposed to do that? There will be nothing left for adhering to Commandment number 2, Love Your Neighbor as God, through Jesus, has loved us! That truly demonstrates our biggest failure in understanding as the Crown of God's Creation! We believe that if we are to give to someone, anyone else what we have will be diminished. That's not how God created us. God created us to realize that everything of real importance exists in an abundance that has no limitation. The more love we share with God, the more love we have to share with our neighbors, brothers, sisters, and even complete strangers.

(After the Young man explained how he had kept the commandments since he was a young boy—)

Jesus looked at him (the Young Rich Man) and loved him. "One thing you lack," he said. "Go, sell everything you have and give to the poor, and you will have treasure in heaven. Then come, follow me."

At this the man's face fell. He went away sad because he had great wealth.

Jesus looked around and said to his disciples, "How hard it is for the rich to enter the kingdom of God!"

The disciples were amazed at his words. But Jesus said again, "Children, how hard it is to enter the kingdom of God! It is easier for a camel to go through the eye of a needle than for someone who is rich to enter the kingdom of God."

The disciples were even more amazed, and said to each other, "Who then can be saved?"

Jesus looked at them and said, "With man this is impossible, but not with God; all things are possible with God." Mark 10: 21-27

The example in this teaching tells us the same lack of understanding. Wealth is not abundance. Being rich does not result in an abundant life. Abundant life only comes from using what you have, to help others live a better life. If you love your wealth more than you love these two great commandments our Lord has given us, you just don't understand. Our abundance is shared with us out of Love, just as Jesus Lived this young man. But we must choose how to share that Love with others. By not meeting this Requirement from Jesus with enthusiasm and a feeling of Great Abundance, the Young Man essentially was saying, I Love God, but I also Love my Riches! How can you make a choice?

Jesus' answer to that question was, there is no choice. If you give your wealth to those in need from a sense of God's abundance, your wealth, though shared with "those less fortunate than you," will be there, now, and forevermore! You see, it's not the wealth that trips us up, it's loving that wealth that we become afraid of losing it. That puts wealth in front of God, and that's our downfall! It's not the money, it's the Love of Money.

My Prayer: Lord of Life and Source of all that we need, we pray that we will not be distracted by the glitter and gold. We realize that our mission as Christians is to share God's Love everywhere, with everyone we come into contact with, continuously without hesitation. Being too attracted by wealth can keep us from sharing as openly and consistently as we know we should. Guide us and protect us as we traverse this difficult road. May we always be focused on your will. AMEN

Day 126: A Devotional for Understanding and Acceptance

Communication is supposedly as free and as open as it has ever been. Not only can anyone publish anything they want at any time they want, but we have access to way too much information that does not meet any known standard for veracity. In fact, some people are so bent on telling falsehoods with such convincing fervor that many people think they must be telling the truth.

So how do we distinguish between truth and fiction. There is one filter that can be used for every statement. That filter is the "Love of Jesus Filter!" Absolutely every single thing you hear, should be able to reflect God's Love as Given us by Christ Jesus! God's Love is full of Grace and Forgiveness. In fact, the only way you will ever find condemnation is by rejecting the Fundamental Love Jesus freely shares with every living human soul. We recognize whether we've accepted or rejected God's Love by how we feel about people we interact with. If we have accepted God's

Love, we feel Joy, Happiness, Abundance, Clarity of Purpose, Health, and Contentment. When we reject God's Love we feel anger, frustration, sadness, agitation, discomfort, and destress.

"So, we have come to know and to believe the love that God has for us. God is love, and whoever abides in love abides in God, and God abides in him." 1 John 4:16 "We love because he first loved us." 1 John 4:19

Let the peace of Christ rule in your hearts, since as members of one body you were called to peace. And be thankful. Colossians 3:15

My Prayer: Lord of Hope and Salvation, we pray that you will help us distinguish between the words and actions that show Love verses the words and actions that reveal our rejection of your Love. Help us to always walk in your Light and share that light with our fellow human beings. May we always remember that we can only serve YOU if we provide that service with a Loving Heart. It is with a Grateful and Joy-filled Heart that we are capable of healing this wounded world. We realize that healing will take place when we openly offer to be the conduit for the Love that will heal our world. Let us show our faith in All we do, for it is. Y Faith that our acceptance of Your Love Becomes REAL! AMEN, Hallelujah, AMEN

Day 127: A Devotional for Understanding and Acceptance

I often look for counter arguments with respect to the Christian Faith. I do this because I was not raised to be a Christian, in fact, I was raised as a blank slate in religion and did not truly get introduced to Christianity until I was entering High School. Our New High School had a small group of teachers that was interested in providing, in an evening , away from campus, a Young Life Program. This is where I had my first introduction to Jesus and how our souls had been ransomed by his crucifixion. I didn't know much, which led to baby questions. I got responses to some of my questions but ended up as a 16-year-old challenging Pastor Weidlich of Grace Lutheran, during my one-on-one confirmation sessions with many questions and probably the most challenging of these I am listing below.

1. How can you tell the voice of God from a voice in your head?
2. How can you tell the voice of God from the voice of the Devil?
3. Would you find it easier to kill someone if you believed God supported you in the act?
4. If God told you to kill an atheist, would you?

These questions often arise in challenges to Christianity, and I knew as a High school Junior I did not have the background in scripture to be able to adequately answer even one of those questions. Pastor Weidlich helped a great deal but through some religion classes in college and through the years of Bible Study, I think I've developed some decent answers to those questions.

1. The voices in our heads tend to be somewhat erratic, and may not always follow the two greatest commandments given by Christ. We know for certain that neither Jesus, nor God the Father, will require us to commit crimes, act with malice against our brothers and sisters, and will always seek outcomes that share abundance, health, and love.
2. The voice of the Devil will not focus on Loving one another without condition. That will be at the center of any message from God.
3. A Christian would never find it easy to kill another human being. It's not a matter of God ever supporting the act of killing another human being, but God understands our imperfections and has already let us know that no sin is too large to be forgiven. He wants us to know that forgiveness requires us to also forgive and to seek a new path forward in the future.

4. It is my belief that God would not direct us to kill people because they are atheists. We have been commissioned by Jesus to make disciples of every nation, religion, race, and in every corner of the planet. This includes atheists and the only way to win over an atheist is through sharing the Love of Christ!

One of the 10 Commandments is: "Do not kill!" Exodus 20:12 There are no "except-when" statements provided. Of course, humans are imperfect and we will, from time-to-time, break very crucial rules. Had we always been perfect, there would have been no need for a Messiah. As for the voices in our head:

John 16:13 When the Spirit of truth comes, he will guide you into all the truth, for he will not speak on his own authority, but whatever he hears he will speak, and he will declare to you the things that are to come."

James 1:19 Know this, my beloved brothers: let every person be quick to hear, slow to speak, slow to anger."

Hebrews 4:12 For the word of God is living and active, sharper than any two-edged sword, piercing to the division of soul and of spirit, of joints and of marrow, and discerning the thoughts and intentions of the heart."

My Prayer: Gracious God, help us realize that the New Covenant is one of Love and Peace. If we are to truly hear your voice, we must listen for the words of unconditional Love, Peace, and Joy that you offer us. There are enough angry and hateful words uttered in our world and far too few words that truly represent the will of God! If we sow the seeds of Peace and Love, there will less space for hate and violence. Lord Jesus: Guide us towards your perfect light! AMEN

Day 128: A Devotional for Understanding and Acceptance

God created everything in a way that is self sustaining and has the potential for perfection. How do we, as part of this perfect creation, move humanity closer to this state of perfection? Every requirement for achieving that universal state has been carefully documented for us in the ancient writings that serve as a guidebook for humanity. If we want to achieve perfection, we need to simply follow those simple straightforward rules.

But humanity, from the very beginning, has rebelled against those requirements. They would rather interpret those words in a way that suits them more favorably than the straightforward, exactly as stated rules. Each of us would be better served by making a personal commitment to these principles and stop worrying about every other human being and what they are doing. Rather than saying, " why doesn't that person just…" we should each say, "here is what I commit to doing!"

Here are my prayers and my commitments for the next several months:

1. I will enjoy my excellent health in every way I can. God has granted me this amazing gift and I will demonstrate my gratitude by living my life to its fullest!
2. I will share my abundance in a way I feel led to share. God has granted me abundant resources so that I might help where I can. I am grateful for these gifts I've been given.
3. God has given me the ability to be a positive influence on others. I will assist others in finding their true purpose and direction whenever they ask. My gratitude for this gift cannot be overstated. Thank you, Lord, for this gift.
4. I will do my absolute best to not judge others. I have no personal idea how anyone else got to where they are. I know only my own starting point and where I've gone on my journey. I am grateful to God for that ability of discernment.
5. I commit to sharing these Devotionals for as long as God keeps giving me the ideas, the words, and the ability to communicate.
6. I will do my best here, and please, hold me to the difficult commitment I am making) I will not judge others, as I know I will be judged, and with the measure I use, it will be measured to me. Why do I look at the speck of sawdust in my brother's eye and pay no attention to the plank in my own eye? How can I say to my brother, 'Let me take the speck out of your eye,' when all the time there is a plank in my own eye? I am a hypocrite, first I must take

the plank out of my own eye, and then I will see clearly to remove the speck from my brother's eye. Matthew 7:1-5 (slightly modified!)

AMEN-HALLELUJAH-AMEN

Day 129: A Devotional for Understanding and Acceptance

Ok, first day after I publicly made my commitments. I am doing pretty well. I've started judging others and immediately reminded myself of my commitment. I need to add to my notion of judging, that I need to be kinder to myself. I am, most often, harder on myself than I am on others. I now know I do this because I am always looking for more and better! I am personally guilty of not allowing my soul to REJOICE!

Our inner being would accept far more, and our response would be much happier if we would just allow our souls to rejoice! We spend too much time focusing we don't have and what's a wrong, that we don't see the marvel, wonder, and miracles God has done in our lives. If we would take the time to appreciate what we have, we might find we are more receptive of future gifts from God. It's Great to give but if you don't gratefully receive, you may not ever have enough to eagerly give. God does not give to those who are not worthy to receive. But if you are truly in a receiving frame of mind, you will find that you're also in a very generous frame of mind. Takers are not receivers and receivers are never in a taking mood!

My Prayer: These situations I place myself in help me narrow my focus and engage my true north guidance system. Gracious God, keep challenging me. As I receive from your abundance, help me maintain my attitude of gratitude and let my inner spirit always be aligned with your Holy Spirit. May Goodness and Mercy follow my aligned connection which keeps me zeroed in on achieving my greater purpose; Lovingly into connection with every person I meet. Let us all see the very critical, unconditional Love you've given us, that we are to send right back out to all our Brothers, Sisters, Neighbors, and even strangers and those we have thought we didn't care for. As we grow in Christian Love, we pray that each person we share Christ's Love with, will in turn share Christ's Love with others! AMEN

Day 130: A Devotional for Understanding and Acceptance

Do you find yourself continuously irritated with national politics? Don't be too concerned. If history tells us anything, we can be assured that the people in power will be replaced by another group as soon as enough citizens realize these rascals don't seem have their best interest in mind! For all of our 224 years of Presidencies, which have seen 45 different people in the office, there have been groups of US Citizens that were certain that the current person in the office was going to lead this country to ruin. President Washington, as our first President, had more latitude in the position than any president since. But Washington had to create the template of how the President should carry out his duties and he agonized over those details. He was his own worst critic!

Since that time, there have always been factions that have vehemently opposed the President and were certain that the nation might not survive. But here we are! 224 years later, the nation is still intact. We've survived a civil war, 2 World Wars, a depression, Presidential scandals, terrorist attacks, Hippies, Cults, and many other calamities! With the Second President, John Adams, the heated and sometimes bordering on violent, political battles began. When he lost his RE-election bid to Thomas Jefferson, many people truly believed that John Adams had undermined the basic freedoms they had fought so hard to attain during the Revolutionary War. And it seems, each subsequent election has been full of venom and discord. Today, with social media, everything looks 10 times(if not a thousand times) worse.

Why do we do this? Why do we let politicians whip us into a frenzy? We put too much trust in people who are willing to say whatever will get people scared and angry enough to believe their point of view is the only one that can ensure domestic tranquility and a prosperous future. BUT WE SHOULD DEFINITELY KNOW BETTER!

Put no trust in a neighbor; have no confidence in a friend; guard the doors of your mouth from her who lies in your arms; for the son treats the father with contempt, the daughter rises up against her mother, the daughter-in-law against her mother-in-law; a man's enemies are the men of his own house. Micah 7:5,6

Thus says the Lord: "Cursed is the man who trusts in man and makes flesh his strength, whose heart turns away from the Lord. He is like a shrub in the desert, and shall not see any good come. He shall dwell in the parched places of the wilderness, in an uninhabited salt land. "Blessed is the man who trusts in the Lord, whose trust is the Lord. He is like a tree planted by water, that sends out its roots by the stream, and does not fear when heat comes, for its leaves remain green, and is not anxious in the year of drought, for it does not cease to bear fruit." The heart is deceitful above all things, and desperately sick; who can understand it? ... Jeremiah 17:5-12

My Prayer: Dear Precious Lord, as we head into another of our constant and continuous election seasons, let us not forget these words from Micah and Jeremiah. Trusting our politicians to be honest with us is like allowing the wolf to herd our sheep or letting the fox guard the hen house. Once our government is in place after each election, we are responsible for following the rules and laws that have been established, even though we know in just a short period of time, the group in power may be turned out of office. Let us trust in your Love and guidance and remember that people are imperfect. Only You alone in your glory as the Creator God, Son of the Living God, Christ Jesus, and the Spirit of the Living God, are perfect. We can and should only place our trust in you. No and forever—AMEN.

Day 131: A Devotional for Understanding and Acceptance

How do we know which leaders to follow? When you know what you believe is important and you expect your leaders to have similar values, it's wry simple, we follow leaders who value the same principles we value. Jesus told us that we would know these people by how they conduct themselves!

By their fruit you will recognize them. Do people pick grapes from thornbushes, or figs from thistles? (Matthew 7:16) As we review what our leaders say and do, we need to hold them accountable for doing what we believe aligns with our values.

So, what are the critical values that Jesus would have us focus on? As we truly think about it, our leaders should want to demonstrate their Love for our Creator God. That is best done through a Loving and caring attention to God's Creation, which includes the People God Created. Of course, the second great commandment is to Love others as Jesus has Loved us. Jesus would ask our Leaders to not so much talk about how much they Love God, but to show how much they Love God through their actions. There are many leaders who talk a good game but do not truly follow what Jesus taught us was important. Jesus called out these leaders and would not give them any credit for being valued leaders.

"They do all their deeds to be seen by others. For they make their phylacteries broad and their fringes long, and they love the place of honor at feasts and the best seats in the synagogues and greetings in the marketplaces and being called rabbi by others. Matthew 23:5-7

My Prayer: Beautiful Savior, Jesus; help us remember what our Leaders should really be like. It's not enough that they say all the things we want to hear, they should, by their example, leave no question as to whether they put others before themselves. And at the top of the list of those they should eagerly place above themselves is our Great Creator God. Help us see through the facade they use to create the allusion of "Goodness, Holiness, and Loving Kindness." If we are fooled by their smooth talking and false promises, we have no one to blame but ourselves. And Lord Jesus, we all realize that neither conservative nor liberal, nor any other political philosophy is without fault. It seems as though those running for office are always more concerned about getting elected than they are with delivering on Christian principle. Help to stop talking Christian Values and Start living by The Christian Values of Unconditional Love. AMEN

Day 132: A Devotional for Understanding and Acceptance

What if I am called to be a leader? How do I conduct myself so that I can remain true to what Christ has called us all to do? "Finally, all of you, be like-minded, be sympathetic, love one another, be compassionate and humble. Do not repay evil with evil or insult with insult. On the contrary, repay evil with blessing, because to this you were called so that you may inherit a blessing. For, "Whoever would love life and see good days must keep their tongue from evil and their lips from deceitful speech. They must turn from evil and do good; they must seek peace and pursue it. For the eyes of the Lord are on the righteous and his ears are attentive to their prayer, but the face of the Lord is against those who do evil."

Who is going to harm you if you are eager to do good? But even if you should suffer for what is right, you are blessed. "Do not fear their threats ; do not be frightened." But in your hearts revere Christ as Lord. Always be prepared to give an answer to everyone who asks you to give the reason for the hope that you have. But do this with gentleness and respect, keeping a clear conscience, so that those who speak maliciously against your good behavior in Christ may be ashamed of their slander."1Peter 3:8-16.

When you witness a leader who behaves differently than what we are told we should be, in scriptures, we know that leader is not emulating Christ. It is understood that all humans have flaws, but the true Christian Leader will always acknowledge their shortcomings. In fact, a Leader that functions in their best attempt to meet true Christian Ideals will be first to acknowledge their mistakes. False Prophets will make excuses, and try to blame others, or simply state that these are such difficult times, no one can blame them for having to take extreme measures to establish order and maintain our freedoms.

When called upon to Lead, set the example! In the face of an out-of-control world, don't exacerbate the situation by behaving in an equally extreme and unchristian way. Be the Light in the darkness. Be that Ray of Sunshine that warms to chilled hearts and souls of people in need. If you lead, do not lead based on who has the most clout, money, influence, or other resources; Make your Leadership entirely based on Integrity. And look for these same qualities in every leader you follow!

My Prayer: Holy Lord Jesus, shine a light on the true qualities of Leadership and help us always select leaders who exemplify what you've taught us. Allow your Incredible, Amazing, Holy Spirit to touch our Hearts, Souls, and Minds in a way that we clearly see the paths we must take. Let us never forget that paths that trample some people, and leave others in ruin and chaos, are not paths of Leadership. Those are paths that end in elitism, discrimination, and favoritism. Help each of us, should we be called to lead, find the way forward that is ruled by integrity, honesty, and inclusion. We thank you for keeping us looking at the world through your fair, equal, and love-based lenses. Without your guidance, we know, things will never get any closer to a Christ-Like society than we have been at any time, over the last several centuries. We patiently seek your direction and road map. Hear our prayer, oh Lord, and keep us safe as we continue our journey. AMEN

Day 133: A Devotional for Understanding and Acceptance

What does the Apostle Paul mean by a living sacrifice? As I read this passage, my inner voice says to be a "Living Sacrifice" we must dedicate our worldly body to serving God's desire for us. Our sacrifice is to stop worrying about the common, daily trappings of our life in this world and devote our personal energy and effort to tasks that ensure that we show our unconditional love to God and all our fellow human beings.

With these words, Paul asks us to pay more attention our spiritual life than we do our physical life. "I appeal to you therefore, brothers, by the mercies of God, to present your bodies as a living sacrifice, holy and acceptable to God, which is your spiritual worship. Do not be conformed to this world, but be transformed by the renewal of your mind, that by testing you may discern what is the will of God, what is good and acceptable and perfect." Romans 12:1-2

When we are so focused, we are actually far richer than we would be if we put all our energies into acquiring Earthly Wealth. By taking our spiritual self seriously, we create a sense of worth and gratitude that creates a most Joyful experience for ourselves and everyone around us. God does not need our gratitude or love, but the Creator realizes that if we practice unconditional Love and having a grateful heart, on the Creator God, we learn how to more purely Love and how to be more appreciative of our fellow humans. With this practice we learn to be more generous, more patient, more open and receptive and with the gratefulness and openness to receiving comes satisfaction like we've never experienced before. It is in these moments that we realize that everything we do produces an outcome. In this way, we have tremendous influence over our futures.

So, whether you eat or drink, or whatever you do, do all to the glory of God. Romans 12:4 By glorifying God, many people are blessed. By glorifying God, many people receive gifts they never knew they could receive.

My Prayer: Gracious God, we pray for patience and that our patience will allow us to appreciate all we have and opportunities for even more success will avail themselves to us! We are grateful for this day and ask your blessing on our futures. Help us create our best future and in so doing give all glory and honor to you.

Day 134: A Devotional for Understanding and Acceptance

What does God want from us? I toiled over my job and worried about every detail and no matter how hard I worked and how successful I thought we were, upon leaving my positions, the new boss would change everything. Today, they are so far away from what I had accomplished, and they have to rediscover some of the same problems and solutions we dealt with 25 years ago! Except, 25 years later, is anything the same? There are very few people in the same positions they were in 25 years ago. None of my children are under the age of 25! Things may look the same, but they are so different, that using every tool we had, 25 years ago, we couldn't even uncover the basis for the problems faced today.

There is always and there has always been, the false notion that we know what the next few generations have to deal with. At the same time, we suffer from nosthesia; that nostalgic look back at how we think life used to be, but it really wasn't like that at all. We've blocked out the truly awful parts of our pasts by reminiscing about how good we think the good parts were, even though the good parts were never as good as we remember them being! Psychological researchers have found that the memories that drive our current behaviors are only about a 50/50 mix of truth and fiction and the further from the event the accuracy of our memory's declines. When we passionately pursue our fondest memories of our youth, we should once again take heed of the words of the Apostle Paul:

So, flee youthful passions and pursue righteousness, faith, love, and peace, along with those who call on the Lord from a pure heart. 2 Timothy 2:2

My Prayer: Lord God, Creator of All things, you gave us Jesus to show how to attain eternal life, yet we reject his straightforward message of "Loving You" and "Loving others" as he has loved us. Help us clarify and simplify our approach to the world. When we Love without hesitation and without condition, we grow closer to you. Giving thanks to you is not something we do because you require it if us, but something we do because it opens our hearts to becoming better people. By being grateful and by loving we become more giving and caring. This is how we become more in tune with creation and the one who created. Al Glory, Praise and Honor to you oh Lord! AMEN

Day 135: A Devotional for Understanding and Acceptance

Can we believe in the power of prayer without trusting God to answer our prayers? The answer to this question is: "It seems like a very common experience of today's Christians!" For many years, when people are asked what they pray for, there is great clarity regarding their prayers. When asked if they believe their prayers will be answered, most say: "absolutely, I have great faith that God answers every prayer." And then several weeks later, if you ask them about the outcomes they hoped for, almost everyone clearly explain why those outcomes are stifled by one or more people or world conditions that prevent those events from happening.

When we consider the ongoing focus of our lives, we see that there are huge resistant beliefs about the nature of our world. This resistance sends mixed messages about what we really want and what we really believe. We say we want to heal our nation, but then believe great evils keep getting in the way of the positive acts of God that will actually heal our nation. Which is correct? God can heal all because God is the most powerful source of Creation there is! Or, evil forces are strong enough to counter the creative forces of Good emanating from God!

If our experience is that God has allowed bad things to continue to happen, we need only to look at where we put our focus. It is not God's lack of power, but our lack of focus on Good. The more we focus on the bad, the more power the sources of evil have. When we pray, let us focus on what we want rather than on what we do not want. Jesus has taught us to pray asking for what we desire, and the doors will be opened!

Paul tells Timothy in 1 Timothy 2:8 "Therefore I want the men everywhere to pray, lifting up holy hands without anger or disputing." Let go of the doubt and despair. Turn to God in total Love, Devotion, and Praise.

"Put to death therefore what is earthly in you: immorality, impurity, passion, evil desire, and covetousness, which is all idolatry." Colossians 3:5

My Prayer: Gracious God, we desire Peace, Joy, and Love of You and our fellow humans! We honor you and raise our voices in songs of praise. Let our Joyous words drown out the hate, anger, deceit, and false narrative. Let us not give any quarter to that which is not of You! Hallelujah Amen!

Day 136: A Devotional for Understanding and Acceptance

Most people today think idolatry ended hundreds of years ago. Certainly, Christians would not have idols today, or would they? What is an idol? An idol is something that humans give equal status when comparing to God! The idol is trusted and honored and worshipped, as though it was God's equal. When God tells us not to worry about what you will wear, or where your next meal will come from, whether your crops will receive rain. Is that what you do? Do you put your worries behind you or do you put your faith in other things?

What agreement has the temple of God with idols? For we are the temple of the living God; as God said, "I will make my dwelling among them and walk among them, and I will be their God, and they shall be my people. 2 Corinthians 6:16

Jesus walked among our ancestors and promises ti walk amongst us again. So these bodies of ours, our temples to the Living God, do we trust them to our God? Or do we worry about how we will be clothed, and fed, and kept safe. Are we relying on other things to meet our needs? These things we think are more capable of providing for us than the Source of all that exists, that source of infinite power, knowledge, and unconditional Love; how can anything else match what God can do for us. But we resist and iOS that resistance that keeps us from receiving the incredible bounty God has promised us!

I challenge everyone to try a little experiment. Starting tomorrow, ask God for one simple, thing. Write down in a slip of paper: write down exactly what you prayed for and the date and time you prayed. Each day for 40 days, at the same time of the original prayer, say a very quick prayer that goes like this: Gracious God, there is no other power in the universe as amazing ad you. I thank you for providing for my needs. And quite specifically, I want to thank you for answering my prayer that I offered up to you on May 16, 2023, at x:xx am. After the 40 days, please note how your prayer was answered.

Here is my Prayer in this experiment:

My Prayer: Gracious God, I ask that you provide me with the ideas that will continue Allow me to write this Devotional for the next 40 days and into the end of 2023. I also ask that the resources needed to keep this going will be abundantly available to me. In addition, I pray that every reader of this devotional series will have their prayers answered as well. Thank you, dear Jesus, for being with us on this journey. AMEN

Day 137: A Devotional for Understanding and Acceptance

How will God be able to provide all that you need and yet be able to provide for me and everyone else? Jesus said to Simon, who he would call Peter, the Rock upon which his Church would be built. He said to them, "Cast the net on the right side of the boat, and you will find some." So, they cast it, and now they were not able to haul it in, because of the quantity of fish. John 21:6

We give Our Great Creator God too little credit for what he is capable of. If God had any hand at all in the creation of our Universe, there is no action he cannot set into motion. It is our fear of "LACK," that keeps us shackled to our small expectation of an infinite God. "Give, and it will be given to you. Good measure, pressed down, shaken together, running over, will be put into your lap. For with the measure, you use it will be measured back to you." Luke 6:38

If Our God is the Alpha and the Omega! If he is infinite, eternal, omnipresent, omnipotent, omniscient Source of All, we should give the Deity we call the Creator, Lord of All, just a little more credit for being able to achieve whatever we ask for. And don't ever worry about being worthy enough, your worth was bought and paid for. The Ransom was extraordinarily high!

For God so loved the world, that he gave his only Son, that whoever believes in him should not perish but have eternal life.

John 3:16

And God is able to bless you abundantly, so that in all things at all times, having all that you need, you will abound in every good work. 2 Corinthians 9:8

My Prayer: Savior Jesus, we ask you to forgive our short sightedness and our lack of ability to allow Our Amazing Creator God to do all he is capable of. It has never been God's inability; it has always been our unwillingness to be fully receptive of the gifts he is willing to give us. We do not understand that gifts are coming our way. Jesus would never have said: seek and you will find; knock on the door and it will be opened for your, ask for it and God will give it to you, if it was not what God really wants to do! Open our eyes so we might see! Open our hearts so that we might Love! Open our minds so that we might truly understand! And we thank You dear Jesus and our

Great Creator God for always listening and providing for our needs! AMEN HALLELUJAH AMEN

Day 138: A Devotional for Understanding and Acceptance

We live in a time when figuring out who really needs help and who the grifters are, has become exceedingly difficult. A few years back, a TV news team followed a man who was panhandling on the street of a major American City using hidden cameras. At the end of the day, the man took a city bus to another neighborhood, got in a car, and drove to a decent neighborhood, pulled his car into the garage, and emerged from the house completely cleaned up with his family. His 9 to 5 job was panhandling, and he was doing quite well with that job! Then there are the people who use the money they get to by booze or narcotics and refuse to get help kicking their habits. And of course, there are the fakes who tell you they are homeless veterans and never served a day in the military. Aren't we justified in turning our backs on these low-life worthless people?

If anyone has material possessions and sees his brother in need but has no pity on him, how can the love of God be in him? — 1 John 3:17

To show that we understand and truly care, we must stick to the teachings of Christ. It will not go well for us if we must face Jesus and defend our actions when he asked us about the times he was hungry, or thirsty or sick or in prison and we did not come to his assistance?

There are ways to help without contributing to their further descent into their own personal pit of pain and suffering. Counselors from the VA ask us to refer people who claim to be veterans to the VA Counseling Services or to the Local Veteran's Service Office. Others should be referred to the Salvation Army, homeless shelters, food banks, free stores, mental health and substance abuse centers. We can make donations to any of these and when we do, rather than turn our back on our brothers and sisters in need, let them know where they can find help.

My Prayer: Lord Jesus, teach us how to show compassion and unconditional Love in these times of great deceit and trouble. Each of us, who has the ability to help must seek your daily guidance so that we do, indeed, help and do not further allow our neighbors, brothers and sisters to continue their downward spiral. I also repeat my prayer from Monday as a reminder to all who read this devotional: I ask that you provide me with the ideas that will continue to allow me to write this Devotional for the next 40 days and on to the end of 2023. I also ask that the resources needed to keep this going, will be abundantly available to me. In addition, I pray that every reader of this devotional series will have their prayers answered as well. Amen

Day 139: A Devotional for Understanding and Acceptance

For centuries, some unscrupulous leaders have purposely made laws, decrees, rules, and even directed their judges to decide against the common people. They've done this to instill fear in the hearts of people and thus control them. During these same years, we the common people, have allowed them to keep us under their thumb. We have always had options that could have released us from their oppression. Isaiah warned those leaders of the consequences that awaited them.

Woe to those who make unjust laws, to those who issue oppressive decrees, to deprive the poor of their rights and withhold justice from the oppressed of my people. — Isaiah 10:1-2

During the majority of this time, people did not have the knowledge or access to information that they could use to change their lives. Even Bibles were read to them and interpreted for them. Up until the early 1800s very few average, everyday citizens could read and they depended on leaders, both community and religion, for information and guidance. We do not have that excuse. Today's access to information and knowledge allows us to change everything. Unfortunately, we've fallen for the myth that there is nothing we can do about our situation. We bought into a story that says, circumstances, people, our past, the stars, fate, or some other external factor in our lives make it too difficult to truly change our future. If that was true, a Caste System would be the best thing for our society.

Fortunately, we've seen a large enough sample of positive deviants to know that not everyone believes that they should, nor do they feel obligated, to stay in their place. We now realize that we can create our own futures and that we are not subjugated to life as something less than others. Within our souls, the Source of All Creation has placed the "spark of Life" which sings Joyously, when our lives are aligned with what God has intended for us. This spark is dimmed when we hate, when we speak hatefully of others, when are envious, when we gossip, or are covetous, and/or are deceitful. We have knowledge, understanding, and opportunity to do things differently. Will we?

My Prayer: Gracious God, help us get aligned with our souls. We need that spark. It is what allows us to be truly, fully alive. We ask for your guidance and support, and we ask that you provide for us all that we need to be able to Love Unconditionally. For it is in Loving that we experience the beauty of this life you have given to us. It is our hope that we will not forget a single gift or blessing provided to us. For we know that it is a grateful heart that serves as a conduit for the blessings that not only will continue to flow to us, but that our hearts will become conduits through which blessings can be provided to ourselves at many others. AMEN

Day 140: A Devotional for Understanding and Acceptance

Every issue you face is truly 2 issues. There's whatever the Bad is you're facing and there's the Good on the opposite side of that coin, which is what you'd like to see! For all the hateful people who make you angry because of how they abuse people you care about, there is the desire you have that they would treat those same people better! If, rather than focusing on the hateful things done, which causes you great pain and distress, you could just as easily focus on all the wonderful things you desire for the people you care about.

The mistake we all tend to make is that we try to change the world by focusing on what we don't want! Here's an example of how looking at what "not to do" can backfire. In the first game of the 1958 World Series, the pitching matchup was classic Warren Spahn for the Braves and Whitey Ford for the Yankees. It was what everyone expected. After 5 and a half innings, the Braves were ahead 2 to 1. With one man on base Hank Bauer came to the plate. Catcher Del Crandall called timeout and went out to the mound. He was followed by the manager Fred Haney. Haney told Spahn, keep the ball low and away from Bauer. He'll hit anything inside out of the park. Upon returning to the game, Spahn is thinking not inside, not inside, not inside. Spahn's pitch belt high on the inside edge of the plate did, indeed, result in a Hank Bauer home run! The lesson of this, your brain does not function in negatives. When you decide that your best action is to "not do X, Y, or Z;" you set yourself up for failure! Focus on what you do want. Where you focus is where you will go!

If we want to make our world a better place, it will have to be through a concerted effort to promote Good, Unconditional Love, Joyful Praise, and Positive Action. For thousands of years we have focused on what we won't tolerate, what's bad, what we fear and what we hate! It has created resistance, rebellion, and more pain and suffering which is only getting worse. There was a reason why Jesus made this statement:

"You have heard that it was said, 'Love your neighbor and hate your enemy.' But I tell you, love your enemies and pray for those who persecute you, that you may be children of your Father in heaven. He causes his sun to rise on the evil and the good and sends rain on the righteous and the unrighteous. If you love those who love you, what reward will you get? Are not even the tax collectors doing that? And if you greet only your own people, what are you doing more than others?

Do not even pagans do that? Be perfect, therefore, as your heavenly Father is perfect. Matthew 5:43-48

My Prayer: Glorious Gracious God, you have given us such good direction yet we seem to continually ignore your truth! We know that we are forgiven by You through the sacrifice of your Son Jesus, but what we really need to do is Forgive Ourselves! Our own condemnation of ourselves gets in the way of us living as fully as you want us to live. Help us to be Joyful in our daily experience! So many of us want the world to make us happy, but we've missed the point! You never said wait a minute, let me make the world a place that is truly pleasing to you and then you can be happy. The world is amazing, and beautiful, and extraordinary enough that every person should be able to find something to be happy about. But that happiness must be in our hearts, souls, and minds before we will be able to recognize it in our world! Thank you for putting all this wonderfulness right there before us. Now it is up to us to find room in our hearts, souls, and minds to allow those joyful experiences in! AMEN

Day 141: A Devotional for Understanding and Acceptance

Sometimes, even though it appears that two options might be on the opposite ends of the very same line, the route to each outcome may not be in the opposite direction from the point where you find yourself. In fact, it is most often true that if you travel in the exact opposite direction from where you don't want to be, you will eventually just get to your least desired location from the opposite side. To avoid this phenomenon, you must head towards your desired destination by traveling in a direction that is anywhere from 45 degrees to 135 degrees in a different direction.

On a Globe that has map markings on it, if you travel at a 45-degree angle relative to an end point you at which you don't want to arrive, and based on where you presently are as a starting point, your destination will be somewhere other than where it is you do not want to be. That's a lot of words to explain the concept of "don't even think about what you do not want!" Keep your focus in the direction of what you do want. If it's a disease you are trying to overcome, it's best to not even think of the disease. As soon as you say "I truly want to do whatever it takes to cure this cancer; you're running a huge risk of your focus zeroing in on the cancer. The opposite of "Cancer"is not "No Cancer." It is best stated as excellent health with a robust immune system.

Similarly, the opposite of poverty is not wealth, nor is it not living in poverty. The opposite of poverty is feeling abundance and having peace of mind. If wealth was the opposite of poverty, anyone that did not achieve their own definition of wealth would be living in poverty. Or, we might say anyone not meeting their definition of being poor would be considered wealthy. But we know that both of these concepts miss the mark. Nor is the opposite of Champion, loser or vice versa!

Finally, brethren, whatever is true, whatever is honorable, whatever is right, whatever is pure, whatever is lovely, whatever is of good repute, if there is any excellence and if anything, worthy of praise, dwell on these things. Philippians 4:8

My Prayer: Gracious God, help us focus on what is true, right, honorable, pure, whatever is lovely, whatever is of good repute, on circumstances that show any excellence, and if anything is worthy of praise, dwell on these things. Help us see our way past the typical bivalent, either-or, black or white ways to view problems and see that they are not always best understood in such simplistic manners. There is so much more about how we deal with our world than just black or white, up or down, yes or no. Help us see the depth of options and opportunities available to us. Thank you for being so patient with us. We are fortunate that your unconditional Love provides the chance for us to remain your blessed children. AMEN

Day 142: A Devotional for Understanding and Acceptance

Are we warriors for Christ? I would gladly be one, as long as everyone adheres to this statement made by Paul and addressed to the Christians at Corinth. "The weapons we fight with are not the weapons of the world. On the contrary, they (our weapons)have divine power to demolish strongholds. We demolish arguments and every pretension that sets itself up against the knowledge of God, and we take captive every **_thought_** to make it obedient to Christ. 2 Corinthians 10:4-5

No guns, no bombs, no tanks, no missiles, no battleships, submarines, aircraft carriers, no swords, knives or bayonets. The weapons of the Warriors of Christ are truth, love, honor, compassion, generosity, and forgiveness! Have you sen seen the popular saying: "Lions, not Sheep!" Have you read how one of the faithful fared against the Lions? So, they went to the king and spoke to him about his royal decree: "Did you not publish a decree that during the next thirty days anyone who prays to any god or human being except to you, Your Majesty, would be thrown into the lions' den?" The king answered, "The decree stands—in accordance with the law of the Medes and Persians, which cannot be repealed."

Then they said to the king, "Daniel, who is one of the exiles from Judah, pays no attention to you, Your Majesty, or to the decree you put in writing. He still prays three times a day." When the king heard this, he was greatly distressed; he was determined to rescue Daniel and made every effort until sundown to save him. Then the men went as a group to King Darius and said to him, "Remember, Your Majesty, that according to the law of the Medes and Persians no decree or edict that the king issues can be changed." So, the king gave the order, and they brought Daniel and threw him into the lions' den. The king said to Daniel, "May your God, whom you serve continually, rescue you!"

A stone was brought and placed over the mouth of the den, and the king sealed it with his own signet ring and with the rings of his nobles, so that Daniel's situation might not be changed. Then the king returned to his palace and spent the night without eating and without any entertainment being brought to him. And he could not sleep.

At the first light of dawn, the king got up and hurried to the lions' den. When he came near the den, he called to Daniel in an anguished voice, "Daniel, servant of the living God, has your God, whom you serve continually, been able to rescue you from the lions?" Daniel answered, "May the king live forever! My God sent his angel, and he shut the mouths of the lions. They have not hurt me, because I was found innocent in his sight. Nor have I ever done any wrong before you, Your Majesty."

My Prayer: Savior Jesus, once again, this daily devotional is a bit long, but how do we leave critical parts of the story out! God has always loved his people, and his people are any and all who love him! And Lord Jesus, you told us directly, and through your disciples, that God Loves all of us unconditionally! If we will but simply allow your Live to guide us and flow through us, there will no longer be a need for weapons of war. We will finally be able to: (He will judge between the nations and will settle disputes for many peoples.) They will beat their swords into plowshares and their spears into pruning hooks. Nation will not take up sword against nation, nor will they train for war anymore. Isaiah 2:4 We yearn for that day oh gracious Lord! AMEN!

Day 143: A Devotional for Understanding and Acceptance

Do you hope for salvation? Or do you know you've been saved? Do you need proof? Or are you sure of the sacrifice made? Are there things you feel you just can't do or are you certain that all things are possible through Jesus the Christ our Lord and Savior.

How we talk to ourselves and other says volume about how we approach our faith and our living of that faith. If we only talk about hope of salvation, we send a message of uncertainty. When we speak of our assurance of being saved we tell world we certain that God Loves us and that because this certainty he will not let us face the ultimate failure. If we talk about what we need, we suggest that God has not provided. This the suggests that without proof of God's Love, we might have the strength of conviction necessary to defend our Savior. Finally, stating that you cannot do something is a direct contradiction of scripture.

I know how to live humbly, and I know how to abound. I am accustomed to any and every situation—to being filled and being hungry, to having plenty and having need. I can do all things through Christ who gives me strength. Philippians 4:12-14.

How can the way we talk to ourselves impact the depth and strength of our faith. Jesus told us ask and it will be given, to seek and we will find, and to knock and the door will be opened for us. If we seek some and only hope we will find, we demonstrate the hollowness of our faith. When seek and fully accept the word of Christ, we will know with surety that we will find what we are seeking. If we ask for something and we do so from the standpoint of need, we make a mockery of God's promise to provide! If we knock on a door and immediately start to think I am unable to what will be required to be worthy of having that door opened for me, we are denigrating the power we've been told Christ has over all of Creation.

My Prayer: Gracious God, Creator of all that exists, we pray that we will move beyond hope to the certainty of your word. And greatest of your word is Jesus our Savior who is: The Word became flesh and made his dwelling among us. We have seen his glory, the glory of the one and only Son, who came from the Father, full of grace and truth. John 1:14 We know that you will provide abundantly, and that you will protect us from disease and injury as we express our faith in demonstrating the behaviors that best show our Love and Faith. And finally, we celebrate your gift to us of influence and Love. Through your power and might, we are blessed with the power of divine Love. Guide us to your altar upon which we will place our gifts of service, support of discipleship, and our talents, strengths, and compassion. We pray this in the name of Jesus, our Lord and Savior. AMEN

Day 144: A Devotional for Understanding and Acceptance

The existence of excellence and the unacceptable, good and bad, smooth and rough, is not evidence of God's indifference to our life experiences. Quite to the contrary, these distinctly different outcomes point out contrasts in our world so that we will know what we do and do not want. Further, we learn over time that some objects and some outcomes seem like they are just what we want at first glance, but upon closer review, we often quickly see the opposite might be more likely to occur. This is one of the reasons that we read in 1st Peter this statement.

"Do not repay evil with evil or insult with insult. On the contrary, repay evil with blessing, because to this you were called so that you may inherit a blessing." 1 Peter 3:9

At the time we may think that the other person deserves our anger and what we intend to do. But we are not really taking an action that will have a huge, behavior altering effect on our rival. In fact, chances are, the other person may not even pay attention to what you say or do. That would be a good response from them. But a more likely response would be for the antagonizer to escalate the conflict and there is a very good chance the situation may begin to impact many aspects of your life.

So, if you are still not sure how to respond to a situation where you feel that another person has "done you wrong, consider this verse from James. "If any of you lacks wisdom, you should ask God, who gives generously to all without finding fault, and it will be given to you. James 1:5

My Prayer: Glorious God of all; we know that you have the power and might to create or destroy. But we also know that you have promised to meet our needs, intercede in our conflicts, teach us when we do not know, and always be our God of All that d Exists. We ask that we be reminded that there is only one eternal judge, and that individual is not made of human flesh and bone. Teach us to desire good, holy and just outcomes and resources. Teach us to know the difference between what we want and what's best for us. Sometimes what we want will result in good outcomes. Other times, what want just might be harmful. And then sometimes the product of what we want is better than we could possibly imagine. Help us to turn to your advice in all our decisions! AMEN

Day 145: A Devotional for Understanding and Acceptance

The power of collective prayer cannot be over stated and should never be underestimated. One intentionally well aligned human being, one person whose soul is intimately connected with the Life Giving Source of Essential Human "Beingness" is more powerful than thousands of negative thinking, misaligned malcontented "non-believers!" To me, these non-believers are people who just won't accept Christ's premise if the two greatest commandments being totally based on love!

Jesus, who was perfectly aligned, is the greatest example of power over the so-called Laws of Nature! Jesus had unconditional, uncompromising Love of All Mankind. He did not differentiate between Jew and Gentile, nor male or female, old or young, rich or poor; he loves us All! A few intentionally, intimately aligned people, we call these people the apostles, changed the course of history. I'm certain that the transformation of our world is not done. We are only waiting for an aligned group of ordinary people, filled with so much Unconditional Love to once again apply that Love to overcome the Laws of Nature!

He (Jesus)went on: "What comes out of a person is what defiles them. For it is from within, out of a person's heart, that evil thoughts come—sexual immorality, theft, murder, adultery, greed, malice, deceit, lewdness, envy, slander, arrogance and folly. All these evils come from inside and defile a person." Mark 7: 20-23

My Prayer: Heavenly Creator God: Help us consider the opposite of this, Let us focus on the Good, the marvelous, the beautiful in our world and in one another. As we change from these evil thoughts, and begin to promote positive, healthy, beautiful thoughts, words and actions, we know we can change this world. Guide us, direct us, give us the strength to commit our hearts, minds, souls, energy, and the totality of our beings to the betterment of our world and everyone in it. Through this we can contribute to the healing of the sick, generating a more peaceful world, and a more abundant existence. Thank you for creating a clean heart in me gracious Lord of All! AMEN HALLELUJAH AMEN

Day 145: A Devotional for Understanding and Acceptance

The power of collective prayer cannot be overstated and should never be underestimated. One intentionally well aligned human being, one person whose soul is intimately connected with the Life-Giving Source of Essential Human "Beingness" is more powerful than thousands of negative thinking, misaligned malcontented "non-believers!" To me, these non-believers are people who just won't accept Christ's premise if the two greatest commandments being totally based on love!

Jesus, who was perfectly aligned, is the greatest example of power over the so-called Laws of Nature! Jesus had unconditional, uncompromising Love of All Mankind. He did not differentiate between Jew and Gentile, nor male or female, old or young, rich or poor; he loves us All! A few intentionally, intimately aligned people, we call these people the apostles, changed the course of history. I'm certain that the transformation of our world is not done. We are only waiting for an aligned group of ordinary people, filled with so much Unconditional Love to once again apply that Love to overcome the Laws of Nature!

He (Jesus)went on: "What comes out of a person is what defiles them. For it is from within, out of a person's heart, that evil thoughts come—sexual immorality, theft, murder, adultery, greed, malice, deceit, lewdness, envy, slander, arrogance and folly. All these evils come from inside and defile a person." Mark 7: 20-23

My Prayer: My Prayer: Heavenly Creator God: Help us consider the opposite of this, Let us focus on the Good, the marvelous, the beautiful in our world and in one another. As we change from these evil thoughts, and begin to promote positive, healthy, beautiful thoughts, words and actions, we know we can change this world. Guide us, direct us, give us the strength to commit our hearts, minds, souls, energy, and the totality of our beings to the betterment of our world and everyone in it. Through this we can contribute to the healing of the sick, generating a more peaceful world, and a more abundant existence. Thank you for creating a clean heart in me gracious Lord of All! AMEN HALLELUJAH AMEN

Day 146: A Devotional for Understanding and Acceptance

For as he thinks in his heart, so *is* he. "Eat and drink!" he says to you, But his heart is not with you.!" Proverbs 23:7

This quote is so true, on so many levels. It is not that people are a certain way and so their thought process is pre-ordained to follow the way they are! If that was "TRUTH," it would be impossible for anyone to change. Change is actually very possible, but not necessarily easy. It doesn't have to be so hard, but we've been duped into believing it's way harder than it needs to be.

For centuries we've known that by adjusting our thinking, we change our lives. Too many people ask for things in prayer and check in the morning to see if their prayer was answered. That's like having faith that a watermelon seed will grow watermelons, but you plant it on Monday and dig it up on Tuesday to see if it has started growing yet. This reveals your lack of belief within your heart! And Jesus was perfectly clears: "If you believe, you will receive whatever you ask for in prayer."

Matthew 21:22 If you pray for your financial situation to improve and you check to see if the money is in the bank the next morning, you are showing how little you trust God with your request. If you really believe, you ask and simply say thank you Gracious Creator God. I believe that you will answer my prayer. And then stop worrying and thinking about it. Trust God!

There are three critical components to seeking God's Loving care through prayer. First is trust God enough to share your needs. He knows what you need but this is simply a circumstance when God want you to be fully aware of what's happening in your world. Next, believe that God will help you find what you are seeking. And the third part is graciously accepting the gift when God gives it to you! This is best done with a grateful heart.

My Prayer: Hear our prayer Oh Lord of All. We each have needs, and we are so thankful for all that you provide for us. Specifically, I ask that I will receive (you fill in your request)… For such a long time you have shown such generosity, as I have so many gifts to be thankful for. With this request, I realize you are fully aware of this need, yet as your Son Jesus told us, we are to ask with a grateful heart. So this is a humble request and before I have even received this Gift I just want say; from the bottom of my heart I want to thank you for the favor you have shown our family. I praise you and honor your name. Amen, Amen, again I say Amen!

Day 147: A Devotional for Understanding and Acceptance

Sometimes, it's best to say nothing, not respond, just listen. Sometimes our silence can speak louder and with more impact than the most well-crafted statement or clever retort. Sometimes that silence, followed by a simple thank you will take us to better outcomes than we might ever have thought possible. "My dear brothers and sisters, take note of this: Everyone should be quick to listen, slow to speak and slow to become angry," James 1:19. "Even a fool who keeps silent is considered wise; when he closes his lips, he is deemed intelligent." Proverbs 17:28 "But let your adorning be the hidden person of the heart with the imperishable beauty of a gentle and quiet spirit, which in God's sight is very precious. 1 Peter 3:4

Jesus spent his life in perfect communion with his creator. He was crucified, died, and entombed, then rose from the dead, not to run roughshod over his detractors but to set an example of how we should bring people to know God, Serve God, and Serve God's Creation. We will never be able to understand what God's people need if we won't be quiet and listen. When God's people speak, too many of us are too eager to tell them what they need to do. It's time to listen. If the Power that created the Universe wanted to, this could all end tomorrow. But that was not the promise. Our Job, as Christians is to: 1) Love God (not because God needs our adulation and fawning, but because we need to know how to Love and how to share his perfect Love, and who better to practice with than God), 2) Love one another, and 3) Make Disciples of Christ in every corner of the world! Making disciples is not a matter of gathering converts. A disciple is: a person having a devoted allegiance to the teachings of one chosen as a master. (Merriam-Webster Dictionary) In this case, the Master is Jesus Christ our Lord and Savior.

My Prayer: Gracious God, Creator of everything, Great and Small, thank you for bringing Jesus to us. Please help us clearly learn the lessons he taught. With his model, we have a perfect plan for solving the problems of our World. If we would but slow down, be quiet, and listen to our fellow human beings, what a difference it would make. We keep learning how but have forgotten to learn WHY. This is the most important lesson. "For you Loved us so much, (even though we continue to go astray and time after time refuse to accept the simplicity of the lesson) You gave your only son, to atone for our unwillingness to simply Love one another, unconditionally, as you asked us to. Once again, forgive us our trespasses as we forgive those who trespass against us! AMEN!

Day 148: A Devotional for Understanding and Acceptance

Sometimes you must speak up! When injustice abounds, it would serve no good purpose to remain silent. When rules are made that make it too difficult for a class, or race, or other unique group of people, to fully participate in activities or privileges that are freely open and available to the dominant group in a community, and if that exclusion puts a group of people at a distinct disadvantage, Christians are expected by their very claim to being a follower of Christ, to speak up for the oppressed and in so doing becoming a defender of fundamental human rights. Among these are life, liberty, and the pursuit of happiness.

"Speak up for those who cannot speak for themselves, for the rights of all who are destitute. Speak up and judge fairly; defend the rights of the poor and needy" Proverbs 31:8-9. "Learn to do good; seek justice, correct oppression; bring justice to the fatherless, and plead the widow's cause." Isaiah 1:17 "But, when we speak up, we should always be aware of how important it is to respect others and to speak gently and kindly." Paul, in his second letter to Timothy, Chapter 2 verses 23-26, tells us:

Don't have anything to do with foolish and stupid arguments because you know they produce quarrels. And the Lord's servant must not be quarrelsome but must be kind to everyone, able to teach, not resentful. Opponents must be gently instructed, in the hope that God will grant them repentance leading them to a knowledge of the truth, and that they will come to their senses and escape from the trap of the devil, who has taken them captive to do his will.

My Prayer: Gracious God, we are often much too impatient in our discussions regarding our Christian Faith, and we can be less than gracious in our disagreements and arguments. Please teach us to treat people as they would like to be treated, rather than as we think they deserve to be treated. Help us understand that to make disciples requires us to be considerate of the sensibilities of those we encounter. Help us be the Christians, you want us to be. We want them to know we are Christians by our Love! AMEN

Day 149: A Devotional for Understanding and Acceptance

Today is Memorial Day. A Day we wish we did not have! In the grand scheme of things, wars are not necessary and only get started because one group of people is trying to exert their will upon another group of people. It is the ultimate failure of the commandment to Love one another. But, through the ages, for many reasons, we have found ourselves in the unenviable position of having to defend ourselves from those who do not like our way of life.

We have called on our young men and women to defend our right to exist as a free society. As we progress through the years, have we always been right in the wars we've fought? From the point of view of the soldiers, sailors, marines, and airmen and women, the ones called upon to make the sacrifice, their belief was yes! In retrospect, we find there are times when other options were available, but the thinking of some leaders was clouded by fear or prejudice or other misconceptions. For the person in the arena of combat, they almost always felt they were doing their duty.

That is why we honor those people who made the ultimate sacrifice by laying down their lives on behalf of a grateful nation.

"As the Father has loved me, so have I loved you. Now remain in my love. If you keep my commands, you will remain in my love, just as I have kept my Father's commands and remain in his love. I have told you this so that my joy may be in you and that your joy may be complete. My command is this: Love each other as I have loved you. Greater love has no one than this: to lay down one's life for one's friends." John 15: 9-13

My Prayer: Holy Lord God, on this Memorial Day, we thank you for the gifts you have given us. None is more precious than the gift of Jesus and his sacrifice on our behalf. Yet, through the years of our nation, our young men and women have been asked to make sacrifices on our behalf as well and we are, indeed fortunate that we have had and continue to have individuals who are willing to make the same sacrifice. The one prayer that says it best simply: ***Thank you God! AMEN***

Day 150: A Devotional for Understanding and Acceptance

Have you seen the candle with this message written on it: This is my last nerve, and it's on fire! Have you noticed that if that is your last nerve, there's no shortage of people standing by with a match! The key in this situation is not to hand out free matches to people!

This circumstance helps us to realize that people who upset you don't need help creating the actions that will set you off. In fact. 99.9% of the time, those irritating people don't even know they are causing you grief and are truly not attempting to do so. There's an old saying: if you don't want people to get your goat, don't let them know where your goat is tied!

One of the most important ingredients in the recipe for happiness is a huge dose of loving yourself so much that it serves as a vaccine against hate, criticism, ridicule, and sarcasm! This may be the vaccine that is most important of all! The immunity it creates results in feeling good about yourself and frees you to unconditionally love others.

"I have told you these things, so that in me you may have peace. In this world you will have trouble. But take heart! I have overcome the world." John 16:33

My Prayer: Gracious God, please vaccinate us with your love, because if we are worthy of your Love, we are certainly worthy of self-love. Show us the amazing rewards that are easily available to those who love and teach us to use that love to forgive and to serve as a guide towards positive, life affirming feelings such as gratitude, a sense of wonderment, and pure joy. AMEN

Day 151: A Devotional for Understanding and Acceptance

Where do you want to go today? I ask myself that question immediately after my morning meditation and prayers. It's not so much about a physical destination, but rather about my mental, emotional and spiritual destination for the day. My most frequent desire is to happily go where I have the opportunity to learn and stretch my human experience beyond where I've been before. This, most often, puts me in a very beautiful spiritual place.

In my years as an educator, I'm sorry to say, way too few people, parents, students, teachers, or administrators, ever truly contemplated this possibility. Too many just wandered about, letting someone else decide where their minds should go, and ignored the emotional and spiritual components of our lives. They were believing they were physical beings that might, quite accidentally, have a spiritual experience.

Jesus brought to humanity the reality of us being spiritual beings that are having a physical, human experience. This is why I ask myself this question every day. In Chapter 6 verse 63 of John, Jesus says: "The Spirit gives life; the flesh counts for nothing. The words I have spoken to you—they are full of the Spirit and life."

My Prayer: Gracious Savior Jesus, teach us to feed our spirit first and then, once we've satisfied our spiritual connection with you and the great Creator, then to fulfill the needs of the body. Help us learn that the emotions of Love, Joy, Peace, and Happiness are great evidence of a contented soul. Once our souls, which house our spiritual being are satisfied, it is so much easier to satisfy the needs of our physical being. Thank you for always teaching us and leading us to a better future. AMEN

Day 152: A Devotional for Understanding and Acceptance

What are your areas of imperfection? We all have them. Sometimes we think we're pretty outstanding in an area that most of our friends think we're not very good in. But truly it's important to realize that everyone has their shortcomings. No one is even close to being perfect. God knows we're well short of perfect and he never expected us to be perfect. If we were perfect there would not have been a need for salvation. And salvation was not needed because of our imperfection, but because we could not accept our own inadequacies and as a rule, we humans always want to blame someone else for our faults. We constantly look for someone to pin the blame on.

We have blamed the poor, the rich, the middle class, the different, the conformists, the trendsetters, the young, the old, the middle aged, the left, the right, the centrist, the uneducated, the college educated, the vocationally educated, the militarists, the pacifists, and so on! However, for the vast majority of our imperfections we have no one to blame but ourselves. As long as we expect someone else to make sense of our world for us, we will be lost. To regain our sense of purpose, which is not to do the impossible, or store up unimaginable riches, or build towers to the moon, we need only accept the fact that without God, God's Power, and God's Creative Energy, our existence is not insignificant, it is impossible.

"You did not choose me, but I chose you and appointed you so that you might go and bear fruit—fruit that will last—and so that whatever you ask in my name the Father will give you." John 15:16

"Have you not known? Have you not heard? The Lord is the everlasting God, the Creator of the ends of the earth. (and as we now know of the ends of the Universe) He does not faint or grow weary; his understanding is unsearchable. He gives power to the faint, and to him who has no might he increases strength. Even youths shall faint and be weary, and young men shall fall exhausted; but they who wait on the Lord shall renew their strength; they shall mount up with wings like eagles; they shall run and not be weary; they shall walk and not faint." Isaiah 40: 28-31

My Prayer: Gracious God, you know we are not perfect! Thank you for your ongoing patience. There are many of us that still think they can fool you. The crazy thing is, we should all know by now, that you have no interest in all of those things we think we need to fool you on! When we read both Old Testament and New Testament verses, we see that what God is interested in is people taking the Commandment to Love one another as seriously as Jesus did! At the point when we get this, money, power, knowledge, skills, talents etc. are of no use in a spiritual world! They only matter in the physical world. So, if we hope to gain spiritual favor by selfishly hoarding our physical gifts, we've missed the mark once again. Guide us back to the right path, Oh Lord if Hosts! We praise you and honor you! AMEN!

Day 153: A Devotional for Understanding and Acceptance

Beware of anyone who professes to know what's best for all people! Beware of anyone who thinks they know what's best for most people! Beware of anyone who says they know what's best for any other person but themselves! "Arrogant know-it-alls stir up discord, but wise men and women listen to each other's counsel." Proverbs 13:10 Don't fool yourselves. Whoever thinks they are wise in this world should become a fool. That's the only way they can be wise. I say this because the wisdom of this world is foolishness to God. As the Scriptures say, "He catches those who think they are wise in their own clever traps." The Scriptures also say, "The Lord knows the thoughts of the wise. He knows that their thoughts are worth nothing." 1 Corinthians 3:18-20

"Not everyone who says to me, 'Lord, Lord,' will enter the kingdom of heaven, but only the one who does the will of my Father who is in heaven. Many will say to me on that day, 'Lord, Lord, did we not prophesy in your name and in your name drive out demons and, in your name, perform many miracles?' Then I will tell them plainly, 'I never knew you. Away from me, you evildoers!'" Matthew 7:21-23

If you think you know what's best for any person other than yourself, beware! Proverbs tells us that if we are arrogant enough to think we know it all, our Lord and Savior will be able to see us for what we are, sham artists. Paul calls us out on these earthly truths and lets us know such knowledge is worthless. Finally, Jesus lays down the ultimate truth! Even if you figure out how to perform miraculous healings, it is all for naught, if we fail at the two critical commands, he gave us; Love God and Love each other.

My Prayer: Amazing Redeemer Lord, help me step beyond my arrogance to fully grasp the importance of Love! Without the deep, abiding, unconditional Love you so lavishly heap upon us, our lives would be so miserable, one could not be expected to garner the energy needed to survive a single day. But you, in all Your Glory provide the energy needed to get through our days with compassion and joy. We know our future is secure and we praise you as we commit to a focus on our role as ambassadors of God's Love. AMEN

Day 154: A Devotional for Understanding and Acceptance

What is Joy? The word comes from the Latin *gaudium, meaning to rejoice, or to be glad in an experience! The French word joie was derived from that, and it was picked up in English as Joy!* What is Hope? In Hebrew, Hatikvah means The Hope. It is more than wishing for a new car or a new job or a pay raise. As believers, we don't just hope without any assurance. Having faith, we can believe that what we hope can be given through Jesus. That is what it means to be partakers of His divine nature.

What is Love? The Hebrew word, Ahava, means love, but this love is incredibly different than most of our contemporary thoughts on love. At the core of Ahava, is the word hav, which means give. This essentially makes this an action concept, rather than a feeling. It's not about feeling great, or warm and soft and comfy. It's about giving to. To give someone something of truly cherished value demonstrates our love. And to give it to them, even though they have not earned it? In its original usage and form, the very concept of Ahava was unconditional Love! Unearned salvation. "For God so loved the world that he gave his one and only Son, that whoever believes in him shall not perish but have eternal life." John 3:16

My Prayer: Gracious Loving God, teach us the concept of "Ahava." To make Love an act of giving something of value to those we care about and even those who do not love us. Help us remember that Jesus admonished those who only wanted to love people who loved them! We are to Love those who hate us as well as those who love us. Help us get past the warm feelings and sought after comfort, so that we can truly appreciate the act of Loving one another as Christ has loved us. Let's spread "Ahava" throughout the world! AMEN

Day 155: A Devotional for Understanding and Acceptance

In 1954, Roger Bannister became the first human to run 1 mile (4 Laps around the standard 440-yard track) in less than 4 minutes. Up until that event, most people thought that was impossible. Since that day, more than 1660 people have achieved that standard. Today, athletes run 1600 meters, which is about 9 meters short of a mile. None-the-less, what I aim to point out is that physical feats, of what are considered impossible tasks, are being accomplished on a fairly frequents basis. To date, 20 high school runners have run the mile in under 4 minutes.

Experts keep saying that certain things are impossible. And we simple humans keep proving the experts wrong. The list of things that experts thought were impossible in the past include things like:

- Space Travel
- Television
- Computers
- Cell phones
- Cloning
- 3D printing
- Running a 4-minute mile
- Airplanes and then people Jumping out of them with a big silk floaty sheet (parachute) keeping the people from crashing into the ground.
- You can add as many as you like!
- One last impossibility: 6 freshmen, 4 sophomore, and a couple of junior girls, earning enough points to place 2nd in the Michigan State Division 2, Track and Field Meet.

I took up this topic today, because a group of 9th and 10th grade girls, today brought home a marvelous 2nd Place Trophy from the Michigan High School Division 2 State Track Meet. These young ladies were up against the best in the state and the truly performed amazingly . We never dreamed they'd come home with that trophy. Somebody forgot to tell these high school students that they weren't supposed to bring home that trophy.

I can do all things through Him who strengthens me. Philippians 4:13–When we stop fighting what God seeks for us and we allow the Lord to display his mighty power through us, we cannot fail. If we enter without heady expectations, only our own humble thoughts, skills, energy and dedication to the task, that allows the power to flow! Don't misinterpret what I'm saying here. It's not that God is on their side. It's that everyone is given certain gifts, but most people never explore the depths of how the gifts they've received might be used! Please, use what you've been given.

My Prayer: Gracious God, help us learn the lesson these wonderful young ladies have to teach us. Focus, use the power and energy given us, do not waver, and seek truth in every opportunity. "But those who trust in the LORD will find new strength. They will soar high on wings like eagles. They will run and not grow weary." Isaiah 40:31 AMEN!

Day 156: A Devotional for Understanding and Acceptance

In recent years, we've heard a great deal about sin, and we've heard a number of different opinions about what sins are worse than any other sin. Once again, I believe we should rely on the one who God sent to us to be ultimate scapegoat for our sins. What does Jesus say about the worst sun we can commit? Here's his answer.

"Therefore, I tell you every sin and blasphemy will be forgiven men, but the blasphemy against the Spirit will not be forgiven. And whoever says a word against the Son of man will be forgiven; but whoever speaks against the Holy Spirit will not be forgiven, either in this age or in the age to come." (Matthew 12:31–32).

The Holy Spirit is how God answers prayers, heals the sick, create new life, solves our problems, and inspires us to be our best for the Good of the world. It is the Holy Spirit that provides the Spark within us that makes life possible. The Holy Spirit can connect with the souls of humans, and if we listen to what God tells us in our heart as it connects with the soul, we will hear the call to Love, which means to give to God and others, without hesitation or condition, from the abundance God has given us.

If we choose to not accept the Holy Spirit, that voice in our heart that repeats the worlds of our Lord and Savior, Jesus the Christ: "But I tell you, love your enemies and pray for those who persecute you, that you may be children of your Father in heaven. He causes his sun to rise on the evil and the good and sends rain on the righteous and the unrighteous. If you love those who love you, what reward will you get? Are not even the tax collectors doing that? Matthew 5: 44-46. If we believe we are accepting the Holy Spirit as our guide and protector, yet we do not trust the power it wields over those who would destroy us, we have, by our actions, rejected the Holy Spirit. Know this, you can believe in the Holy Spirit, but Our Savior has already told us that what we do is far more important than what we say!

My Prayer: Heavenly Creator God, we sincerely hope that we can demonstrate our true faith and Love of you by what we do. We pray that our actions will be pleasing in your eyes and that if we should ever slip in our acceptance of your Holy Spirit, that you would guide us back to a more perfect communion with your spirit within us. We pray that the people we know of who are battling disease, disasters, violent acts, the acts of dishonest people, or any other difficulty, will find comfort, peace, and healing. Send your Holy Spirit to intercede on their behalf. Heal them, comfort them, and Hold Them in your Loving Arms. Let them know how real and amazing the Spirit of the Living God is. Today, Tomorrow, and Forever! HALLELUJAH AMEN!

Day 157: A Devotional for Understanding and Acceptance

How do we truly change our hearts, minds, and source of our daily sense of direction for our life? It requires awareness in all aspects of our existential experience coupled with an intentional act during each experience. We live out each day with 95-99% of our thoughts, words, deeds, and feelings occurring on autopilot. Our habits of mind and feelings run our lives. We become prisoners to our past and each waking moment passes us by without any real plan to face that moment with an intentional thought, word, action, or feeling!

How we face the world each moment is built upon how we interpret the data and observations we make on a moment-to-moment basis. Since there are millions of inputs into our nervous system each day, if our brain and body tried make sense of all of it, our brains and bodies would most likely shut down from sensory overload. So, our brains and bodies, based on how we have previously decided about the value of each type of stimulus, filters, sorts, and recognizes or rejects hundreds and thousands of pieces of information each day. If our interpretation of veracity and value is not in our own best interest, we can make decisions and take actions that can be harmful to ourselves, to others, or sometimes both.

The cure for this problem is mindfulness. Mindfulness is a personal practice that requires us to take our lives off autopilot and carefully consider why we do what we do and seek to understand the nature of any bias or prejudice that might influence our actions. So, with that in mind: the What does the Bible teach about mindfulness?

Blessed are those who have learned to acclaim you, who walk in the light of your presence, Lord. They rejoice in your name all day long; they celebrate your righteousness. Psalm 89:15-16

You make known to me the path of life; in your presence there is fullness of joy; at your right hand are pleasures forevermore. ~ Psalm 16:11

But when you pray, go into your room, close the door, and pray to your Father, who is unseen. Then your Father, who sees what is done in secret, will reward you. Matthew 6:6 "And I will ask the Father, and he will give you another advocate to help you and be with you forever—the Spirit of truth. … You know him, for he lives with you and will be in you." ~ John 14:16-17

My Prayer: Great Creator of All we have and can experience, awake in our hearts the true desire for truth. It's far too easy to just accept our experience as the reality for all. But, what we think is truth, is most often a skewed view of our own experience, and most often a deviation from what a disinterested 3rd party would report as what actually happened. Bring us back to the point of inquiry and away from our false sense of certainty. This will open our minds, our hearts, and our sense of wonder in you. If the human race is ever to truly come to grips with our relationship with you and the rest of humanity, we must understand the flawed premise we all build our "Truth" from. Let us realize that we can only approach truth through the concept laid out in the passage from John, quoted above: "the Spirit of truth. ... You know him, for he lives with you and will be in you." AMEN

Day 158: A Devotional for Understanding and Acceptance

Today is a "Brand New Day!" Today, God is with us, whether you want God to be with you or not, God is here. His Holy Spirit is in your Heart, directing your inner being, your soul, to behave in a way consistent with the Unconditional Love The Holy Spirit brings to us. Can you imagine, what would happen, if at the very same time, every person, in the entire world, would tune into the spirit of the Life Source Offered to us by our Loving and Gracious God! Oh For 8 Billion Voices to Praise God at the same moment! What an incredible song that would be!

You may say, that's not possible; it's never going to happen. It's not that it's not possible. It's that this world has a very strong pull. This world creates the illusion of loss, when it's really a massive gain. It's a point when we gain all the freedom granted us in heaven while we are still living. From that time Jesus began to preach, saying, "Repent, for the kingdom of heaven is at hand." Matthew 4:17 If we will simply acknowledge the fact that we are imperfect. That we ignore the the voice of God within us. That we so want to do it all by ourselves that we refuse to allow our souls to guide us. Our souls, that Holy Spirit Guide within our Hearts, that is our personal connection with The Creator God.

"Now when He was asked by the Pharisees when the kingdom of God would come, He answered them and said, 'The kingdom of God does not come with observation; nor will they say, See here!' or 'See there!' For indeed, the kingdom of God is within you.'

Then He said to the disciples, 'The days will come when you will desire to see one of the days of the Son of Man, and you will not see it.'" Luke 14:20-22

My Prayer: Gracious Holy God, we ask that we can focus our Hearts, Minds, Souls, and Actions on your Kingdom within us. The power we will generate will be as though every electrical power plant in our world, suddenly connect to one powerful beam of Love and spread it throughout the world. The Power of Your Love has never been needed more than it is needed right now. Guide us to that perfect light of Love, Peace, Hope, and Faith. We have, within ourselves all that is needed to change our world. Our Glorious God in Heaven, no power is greater than You. Your Kingdom is within us. Let Your Will wash over us. Here, Today, in our everyday existence as it will when we join you eternally. Give us from your abundant resources, all that we truly need. And forgive us for blocking your will in the past in the same way we have forgiven those who have blocked us out of our connections with them. Please lead us away from our selfish behaviors, for we know these keep us from accepting your Love. For Your Kingdom is what we truly desire as nothing can generate more amazing love and caring compassion than you. AMEN

Day 159: A Devotional for Understanding and Acceptance

Where do you put your attention? Notice I said, Where do you Put, not what do pay attention to. Attending is a choice. You may have heard that 90% of success is just showing up! In life, attendance is not optional. To live you must be there. If you're going to be there, you might as well put your attention on the ideas, things, and actions that help you, rather than on the things that can potentially harm you.

Many people think they are doing just that. They say I'm trying to solve problems. But while focusing on the problems, the problems suck the energy, joy, and happiness right out of you. To do the most good anyone can do, you we must put our attention on those things that bring a satisfied sigh to our souls, rather than the gasp of exasperation that is all too common these days. So how do you create a satisfied soul? Look to the Epistle of James Chapter 4 vs 1-3: What causes fights and quarrels among you? Don't they come from your desires that battle within you? You desire but do not have, so you kill. You covet it but you cannot get what you want, so you quarrel and fight. You do not have because you do not ask God. When you ask, you do not receive, because you ask with wrong motives, that you may spend what you get on your pleasures.

This points out 3 reasons our souls are not at peace and become dissatisfied. 1) we desire things that we will not ask God for, 2) we are envious of what other people have, 3) we desire things that if we receive them, they might hurt others or, at the very least we desire them with no concern for the consequences and impact of our actions on others. Our souls are satisfied when we see that what we say, think, and do is pleasing to many but most of all pleasing to our creator. It's not that we're being selfish, it's that we are too often not even considering the impact of what we do. Although the act may bring some initial pleasure, in the long run, these inconsiderate acts are not satisfying.

My Prayer: Gracious God, hear our prayer. We know we are often asleep at the wheel, and this is usually after insisting we can do this by ourselves. Forgive us for our impertinence. How we can possibly believe we can handle all of this through our earthly form is just about as silly as we can get. Guide us back to the path that truly leads to understanding. If we focus our attention on those things that bring peace and satisfaction to as many people as we possibly can, we will know we are on the right track. Bless us with your gentle guiding hand and let us bask in your undying unconditional Love. AMEN

Day 160: A Devotional for Understanding and Acceptance

How do we change our world? It seems like every generation has a desire to change the world but they all come up short. Why is that? Yesterday I wrote about where we put our attention. Granddaughter Tessa is taking Drivers Training. She's learning quickly, that where we put our focus, that's where the car goes!

"A change, it had to come   We knew it all along

We were liberated from the fold, that's all

And the world looks just the same   And history ain't changed

'Cause the banners, they all flown in the last war" Written by Peter Townsend of Who 1971. The Title of the song: ***Don't Get Fooled Again***!

Here we are! Fooled again! It happens over and over and over! Meet the new boss, same as the old boss! Who's Your Boss? Really, who's your boss? As long as my boss continues to be anyone other than the eternal being within my soul, that connector to the Creator, my song will continue to be "Don't get fooled again!" The Album, Who's Next, had another song that resonated with a number of Baby Boomers, "My Generation." In each case, our focus keeps returning to people or a person. Real change cannot be imposed upon us. We must find that essence of the Holy Spirit within our souls and embrace it. This will connect us to our Beautiful Savior, Ruler of All Nations!"

The New Boss is human, same as the old boss! Unless you put the human bosses aside and allow the Eternal, Forever, Always New Boss, who is Always Exactly the Same As the Eternal, Forever, Always Old Boss, to be your One and Only Boss!

"When the Spirit of truth comes, he will guide you into all the truth, for he will not speak on his own authority, but whatever he hears he will speak, and he will declare to you the things that are to come." John 16:23

And how will you know the Spirit of truth when you sense the direction you are being led?

105

The Apostle Paul tells us one way we will know: I speak the truth in Christ—I am not lying, my conscience confirms it through the Holy Spirit—Romans 9:1 A few other ways are explained by the Prophet Joel: "And it shall come to pass afterward that I will pour out My Spirit on all flesh; Your sons and your daughters shall prophesy, your old men shall dream dreams, your young men shall see visions; and also on My menservants and on My maidservants I will pour out My Spirit in those days." (Joel 2:28-29)

There is one absolute certainty, the Holy Spirit will not instruct us to do anything, that violates God's Laws of Loving God and Each other. We are assured of God's undying devotion to the Creation.

My Prayer: Gracious Glorious God of the Universe, we ask you for a better understanding of our connection to you through the Holy Spirit. There are many imposters, and though we may want to be constantly listening for your voice, we are concerned that we might be reading our signals wrong. Teach us how to know the difference between the Good and the purposely deceptive. Even though we are certain that we will never be led into evil, there are so many deceivers out there, it gets harder and harder to tell the difference. We ask that we will be able to determine which is Good and which are not so Good. Help us realize that none are as Good as their staunchest supporters claim them to be and none are as evil as their archenemies claim they are. We ask for the Peace that passes all understanding and that kindness and joy will prevail! AMEN

Day 161: A Devotional for Understanding and Acceptance

Have you asked yourself, why haven't I received what I asked God for? Jesus said, ask and it will be given yet I still do not have it! What's up with that?

There is a very simple reason for this and it is so common, most people just can't believe it's true. When we ask for something, let's just say you've asked for a new job that will be more to your liking than your current job. You'd like it to have fewer hassles from your supervisor, less mandatory overtime, and better wages and benefits. After asking for this, the most common thought process is to continuously compare every new opportunity to the old situation. By doing this we are so focused on what we don't want than what God has to offer us, we continually reject what God sends our way out of fear that the new job won't be any better than the old job. We quickly demonstrate our lack of faith. We become Peter, walking on the water. As soon as we realize what we're doing, we abandon our faith!

How do we possibly keep our faith when we are so afraid of repeating our past? Focus on what we want without giving a moment's thought to what we do not want. God knows why we desire the change, but we constantly throw the past at the situation and every saving prospect that is sent our way we reject out of fear that the new will be no better than the old! To have better news, we have to make the new better. See the greatness of the new and celebrate it, honor it, love it for what it is. We all too often start to put our own twist on the new and since our experience was the old, we start to transform the beautiful new into the ugly old situation!

"No one sews a patch of unshrunk cloth on an old garment. Otherwise, the new piece will pull away from the old, making the tear worse. And no one pours new wine into old wineskins. Otherwise, the wine will burst the skins, and both the wine and the wineskins will be ruined. No, they pour new wine into new wineskins." Mark 2:22 When Jesus said this, he was telling his followers, not to compare him and what he does to anyone else. His ways are not the same as the way of any other. His new way focuses only on the Good, Loving, and Holy. When we compare the new situation to the old, we are telling Jesus, just make my old situation better and I'll feel good. And Jesus is saying have faith, demonstrate that faith through loving what God gives you, and your situation will be beautifully better. You must Love the life you've been given first, then your life will become the life you love and the situation of your life will be better.

My Prayer: Wonderful, amazing savior, we want to thank you for sending your Holy Spirit to us so that we can truly Love ourselves and the life you've given us. Your sacrifice has been the type of joyful experience that sets us apart from those who do not have faith. You keep us from sinking when we are called to walk on the water. You give us new cloth to patch our old worn souls and new wine skins to hold the new wine which is our reborn spirits. It would be useless to patch our torn and tattered souls with the same old cloth that so easily ripped. And what good would our new spirits be if we put the Joy to the weak old skins that have let us down before. Bless us Dear Savior Jesus, for we crave and desire the goodness you create in our Souls. AMEN

Day 162: A Devotional for Understanding and Acceptance

Have you noticed that we can be led in some amazingly positive directions by some very unlikely people. Through the ages, God has taken some of the most unlikely people and used them to lead significant groups of people towards a deeper faith. The most difficult part of this for most of us is how do we differentiate between someone who is truly sent by God, and those who are usurping a piece of the message for their own purposes. These false prophets are almost always very convincing but there are definite telltale signs of their deceptive nature.

But the Lord said to Samuel, "Do not consider his appearance or his height, for I have rejected him. The Lord does not look at the things people look at. People look at the outward appearance, but the Lord looks at the heart." 1 Samuel 16:7

Brothers and sisters, think of what you were when you were called. Not many of you were wise by human standards; not many were influential; not many were of noble birth. But God chose the foolish things of the world to shame the wise; God chose the weak things of the world to shame the strong. God chose the lowly things of this world and the despised things—and the things that are not—to nullify the things that are, 1 Corinthians 1:26-28

Now when the men of the Sanhedrin (Jewish High Court) saw the confidence and boldness of Peter and John, and grasped the fact that they were uneducated and untrained [ordinary] men, they were astounded, and began to recognize that they had been with Jesus. And seeing the man who had been healed standing there with them, they had nothing to say in reply. Acts 4:13-14

All through both the Old and New Testaments of the Bible, we see ordinary men and women confronting the leadership of the day. Boldly taking God's Word to let the world know that the Brash, Loud, Brazened, Powerful people are not the ones who really are the true leaders in God's Great Plan. It is the unlikeliest of the People who understand with incredible humility, that lead us in the only way that matters. If you want to get to the head of the only line that counts, you must be willing to put yourself last, behind all others.

Jesus called them together and said, "You know that the rulers of the Gentiles lord it over them, and their high officials exercise authority over them. Not so with you. Instead, whoever wants to become great among you must be your servant, and whoever wants to be first must be your slave-- just as the Son of Man did not come to be served, but to serve, and to give his life as a ransom for many." Matthew 20: 25-28

My Prayer: God of All Creation, how we all want to be great and influential and powerful! Yet you Guide us through the voices of ordinary people. Jesus did not come riding in the most luxurious mode of transportation, he came on the back of a donkey. He was not wearing a Golden Crown and fancy robes; he was in the clothing of a common man wearing a crown of thorns. Yet we keep listening to the Loud and Proud! Forgive us, for we truly do know what we are doing! Help us become nothing so that we can finally be of great use to You! AMEN

Day 163: A Devotional for Understanding and Acceptance

Over the years, the rainbow has been a sign of hope, promise, mercy, and redemption. It has been part of almost every mythology of humankind. It has been seen as evil as well as amazingly good. Rainbows were the cause of children disappearing and revealing great riches if you could only find the end of the rainbow. And if you could only fly over the rainbow, life would become as nearly perfect as it could possibly be. Scientifically, rainbows are caused by sunlight passing through raindrops revealing the colors of the visible spectrum.

And God said, "This is the sign of the covenant I am making between me and you and every living creature with you, a covenant for all generations to come: I have set my rainbow in the clouds, and it will be the sign of the covenant between me and the earth. Whenever I bring clouds over the earth and the rainbow appears in the clouds, I will remember my covenant between me and you and all living creatures of every kind. Never again will the waters become a flood to destroy all life. Whenever the rainbow appears in the clouds, I will see it and remember the everlasting covenant between God and all living creatures of every kind on the earth." Genesis 9: 12-16

In the 1960s and continuing through the 70s, 80s, and 90s the Reverend Jesse Jackson, initially by the request of Dr. M.L. King, created the Rainbow PUSH (People United to Serve Humanity) Coalition. The purpose was to bring every cultural and ethnic group together with the mission to protect, defend, and gain civil rights by leveling the economic and educational playing fields, and to promote peace and justice around the world. In this situation the rainbow represented the tremendous variety of people that are found all over America and throughout the world.

Over the past few decades, the Rainbow has been adopted as a symbol of the LGBTQ … movement, primarily to bring attention to the ill-treatment of this group of people. There are numerous people who ridicule and berate this usage of the rainbow as a symbol for this movement, just as people ridiculed and berated the Rainbow-PUSH Coalition. Let's talk about why there should never be a need for these controversies and how to change the circumstances so that there would not be these battles. These controversies and battles have occurred as a result if some individuals believing they have not only the right but the duty to correct these groups! They are lazy or sinful and will not amount to anything worthwhile without our correction of their misguided lives! Isn't this what Jesus would do?

My Prayer: Gracious Jesus, you told us that there was only one sin that could not be forgiven. You said Even denying him could be forgiven. But, denying the Holy Spirit, that is unforgivable! In Mark 3: 28-30, we read: "Truly I tell you, people can be forgiven all their sins and every slander they utter, but whoever blasphemes against the Holy Spirit will never be forgiven; they are guilty of an eternal sin." He said this because they were saying, "He has an impure spirit." And if Jesus was willing to forgive the woman at the well, and the woman who was going to be stoned for adultery, what right have we to treat anyone as anything less than worthy. It is presumptuous on our part to condemn those that Jesus would not condemn himself! Help us forgive others of their shortcomings, in hopes that we too will be forgiven. I am so sorry for the many times in the past that I have spoken badly of those I did not understand. Forgive me of this dear Jesus and guide us in our daily lives so that we can be better stewards of all we've been given and so that we may lead more to your kingdom. AMEN

Day 164: A Devotional for Understanding and Acceptance

I have been asked, several times, do you ever run out of ideas and really struggle for a topic for your daily devotion? The answer to that question has 3 parts to the answer. First, seeing as it is not my devotional, I can't run out of topics for my devotional. Second, there will always be topics of importance in this world. People keep trying to speak in place of or for God, and God needs neither of those. And as people try to usurp God's Word to fit their own purposes, I have a constant supply of ideas. And third, God will not let me quit. As soon as I think the well has run dry, I hear the resounding voice in my head saying; "Oh Ye of Little Faith. How could you think you'd get off that easy?" When you start a conversation with the one in charge, you don't get to decide when the conversation ends.

Occasionally, I wonder why, God allows me to do dumb things. Finally, I figured it out, God is not allowing me to do these things, I'm doing these things because I'm ignoring the guidance provided. I know that if I eat my food too fast, I might bite my lip, or cheek, or tongue; but I'm in charge of that and I end up paying the consequences. Aren't we all the same? Don't we all rebel at the most inopportune times. And isn't it interesting that just at the time I'm thinking I've run out of things to write about that God would allow these thoughts to creep into my head.

The Holy Spirit is truly amazing. If we <u>just listen,</u> we will have the guidance we need, to have our best life possible. That is what God wants for every one of us. "But when he, the Spirit of truth, comes, he will guide you into all the truth... he will glorify me because it is from me that he will receive what he will make known to you. "John 16:13-14.

My Prayer: Gracious Lord of All Creation, thank you for giving us the best advice ever. We know we are obstinate, and want to do things our own way, but when we quiet our thoughts down, we can sense your words clearly. It is always advice that is consistent with what Jesus taught and we can find the best support for the direction we receive. We need only confirm what we are told by reading your word. It is indeed a light unto the best our lives can be. AMEN

Day 165: A Devotional for Understanding and Acceptance

When you observe people, do you notice how some people go about their daily activities with tremendous confidence and are successful in most of their endeavors, while others struggle to get through the day? Can we guarantee that we will be confident and successful people and not an individual who struggles? The answer to that question is yes, as long as you realize that as you move forward, for every question you ask, and every action you intend to take, there is only one answer! The answer: Step Back, get out of your own way! Let Go and Let God take charge!

In their hearts humans plan their course, but the Lord establishes their steps. **Proverbs 16:9** You will keep in perfect peace those whose minds are steadfast, because they trust in you. **Isaiah 26:3** And we know that in all things God works for the good of those who love him, who have been called according to their purpose. **Romans 8:28**

"Therefore, I tell you, do not worry about your life, what you will eat or drink; or about your body, what you will wear. Is not life more than food, and the body more than clothes? Look at the birds of the air; they do not sow or reap or store away in barns, and yet your heavenly Father feeds them. Are you not much more valuable than they? Can any one of you by worrying add a single hour to your life?" Matthew 6:25-27

My Prayer: Holy Creator of all that is known and all that is yet to be known. We thank you for your unconditional Love and for all you have given us. As was the case in ages past, we continue to struggle, not because you want to teach us some lesson, but because we won't pay attention to the plans you've set in our own hearts. You show us despair and joy so that we can see the what leads to each. But we look for how to avoid despair rather than how to create Joy. By focusing on what creates the bad, we create it. As we know in our hearts and souls, where we place our focus, is what we create. Help us place our FOCUS CLEARLY AND INTENTLY ON WHAT CREATES JOY! AMEN

Day 166: A Devotional for Understanding and Acceptance

Today's devotional and each day for the rest of June is dedicated to experiences in this world that I find so awesome, that I will definitely say I am for that! My wife's smile, as well as the smiles that I so often see on my children, their spouses, and my grandchildren, I am also 100% for kindness. There is so much in this world that people find to be against, yet those things are always divisive. When we try to eliminate everything, we don't want or like, we create two ends of a spectrum that cannot bring our world peace. Jesus desires that we focus on that which brings people to him. The soft, warm, loving smiles of those who have captured our hearts are one of those things that unites.

Over the nearly 60 years I've known my wife, I've seen her turn sad children, rancorous teenagers, and angry adults to dearest friends who never forget the kindness she has shown. It is amazing how often we see an adult, often well into their 40s who will introduce Barb to their spouse and frequently their own children, as the best teacher they ever had. She has a way with kids! She truly loves them. She knows how to turn a child's anger, sadness, frustration, disappointment, or other negative mood, in the most constructive direction possible. Her ability to redirect negative energy towards a more constructive energy is amazing. That belief in the possibilities is so refreshing; I've often wished we could bottle it and pour it out on the world.

Each of our grandchildren have acquired a bit of their "Nana." We observed them delivering this kindness when they could have easily just walked away. They've been influenced by the conduit that connects those grandchildren to her, our kids and their spouses. The Motto of Barb has always been "Kindness Matters!" No matter what the circumstance, kindness always has a better chance of generating a more positive outcome than any other approach.

"Blessed are the merciful, for they will be shown mercy." Matthew 5:7 At the core of kindness is mercy. And as Peter reflects on how mercy plays out in our Christian experience: For this very reason, make every effort to add to your faith, goodness; and to goodness, knowledge; and to knowledge, self-control; and to self-control, perseverance; and to perseverance, godliness; and to godliness, mutual affection; and to mutual affection, love. 2 Peter 1:5-7. And Paul tells us:

Little children, let us not love in word or talk but indeed and in truth. 1 John 3:18

My Prayer: Savior Jesus, guide our steps towards kindness. We desire to be merciful so that we may be shown mercy. We desire to turn our loving and positive thoughts and loving and positive actions. There is far too much hatred, anger, and distrust in our world. Let us, your children, be the purveyors of peace, love, and kindness in our world. In the words sung by Dionne Warwick: What the world needs now, is Love Sweet Love, that's the only thing that there's just too little of!" AMEN

Day 167: A Devotional for Understanding and Acceptance

Continuing with the theme I set for the remainder of June, I'd like to mention these three topics: discovery, learning something new, and living life to its fullest. Each of these requires that we tune in to wavelengths that Carry messages associated with each idea. If you'd like to listen to a radio broadcast of your favorite baseball team, you can't do that by tuning into a station that only plays classical music. You must find the frequency of the message you want to hear.

Discovery requires a very open mind. The frequency of an open mind does not block out messages that are strange, or uncomfortable, or unheard of. From 1982 to 1986, I was the science department chair at Carl Sandberg High School in Orland Park, Illinois. One of my Chemistry Teachers had really made a name for himself before I was even on board. He thought of himself as the most knowledgeable Chemist around. A student in one of his classes, came to class one day, with a strange photograph. He showed it to this chemistry teacher and told him his father had taken an electron micrograph of a water molecule. This teacher promptly told the student is was rubbish because it was impossible to take a photograph of something so small. The young man's father was Dr. Albert Crew, one of the foremost developers of advanced electron microscopy and inventor of the scanning transmission electron microscope. As chair of the physics department at the University of Chicago, he had won numerous awards. His work led to the development of semiconductors, which if not created, we'd still have computers that needed vacuum tubes and rooms that took entire office buildings to do their work. lap Top computers and Cell phones would not exist.

Over the past 40 years, what we are learning has increased exponentially. If we had continued the close minded, that's impossible attitude we would have fallen so far behind the rest of the, catching up would be difficult at best. Being close minded to the unusual, unheard of, and thinking you know more than one else in the room, will keep us from Living Life to the Fullest. "I have said these things to you, that in me you may have peace. In the world you will have tribulation. But take heart; I have overcome the world." John 16:33

"Humble yourselves, therefore, under the mighty hand of God so that at the proper time he may exalt you, casting all your anxieties on him, because he cares for you." 1 Peter 5:6-7

My Prayer: Gracious God, we make our greatest progress when we open our hearts and open our minds. When think we have it all figured out and that change is out of the question, we insult the greatest human change agent ever, your only Child, Jesus. Of course, had you decided that the universe was fine as it is, the greatest change ever, Creation, would not have happened. Throughout the Old Testament you provide evidence of your corrective actions and noted that people who were part of nations previously rejected were now in great favor for their faith and devotion to You. When we harden our hearts and minds, we move away from the dynamic universe you created us to manage. Forgive us, redirect us, and energize us toward a more aligned and abundant life. AMEN

Day 168: A Devotional for Understanding and Acceptance

Every human being is moving. How far they move on any given day, in relationship to where they started, depends on how receptive and appreciative they are regarding the possible destinations of the road they are traveling. The rate at which we travel and the intensity of the of the drive we feel pulling us towards the destination, create the momentum we experience in our life. What we sometimes get wrong in this process is not understanding that destinations generate a magnetic attraction and what we focus on is always what pulls us onward. If there is something you do not like, and therefore you do not want, if you try to avoid the road that leads to that destination, the energy generated by the attempted avoidance increases the power of the attraction towards the unwanted road and its destination.

Changing the Momentum of your life requires patience, the deepest compassion for yourself and others, and a determination to find joy on the roads that lead to your most desired destination and in every other part of your day! Just because you may have taken a so-called "wrong" turn does not mean that there is no joy to be experienced. Some of the greatest discoveries in human history have come due to the serendipitous results of what many would have been failed endeavors.

One of the biggest medical discoveries was the antibiotic Penicillin. If Alexander Fleming had just thrown out his spoiled Petri dishes, we'd never discovered the antibiotic. And if Percy Spencer had not noticed a chocolate bar was melted by the energy from a radar test, we might not have microwave ovens. Other serendipitous discoveries were Vaseline, plastics, the strikable match, and gun powder. And anesthetics, such as nitrous oxide (laughing gas) resulted from noticing that people felt no pain when exposed to it and falling safely asleep!

The journey we are on is not an experience that is without Joy. We must look for the joy that is part of every step along the way. "Then you will experience God's peace, which exceeds anything we can understand. His peace will guard your hearts and minds as you live in Christ Jesus." Philippians 4:7

"This is the day the Lord has made. We will rejoice and be glad in it." Psalm 118:24

My Prayer: Gracious Creator God, teach us to be content while still moving forward. Contentment does not have to mean just stop moving because everything is just the way it should be. Contentment is, most definitely, finding your love in every situation. We put ourselves in some difficult places, yet you do not abandon us. We look up after hanging our heads, and if we look carefully enough, we will recognize you in our world. It is you that we are ultimately attracted to; you are the source from which all came and to which we will all return. The road will only be smoother if we stop focusing on the difficulties and place our focus, hope, and faith on your never ending, unconditional Love! AMEN

Day 169: A Devotional for Understanding and Acceptance

This is the fourth day in my series of "things I am for!" Today I am stating that I am definitely, without a single doubt, very much in favor of beauty wherever it's found! Part of my reason for this series is that when we find an incredibly large number of things we can be in favor of, the multitude of positives can be used to tamp down the ongoing emergence of the negatives that keep our strength of God's Love at a very Low Level. If we want God's Live to make a positive difference in our lives, we need to allow those Loving Strands of Light to penetrate as much of our souls as possible. When we start to look for the bad in people, rather than the good, we shift our personal responsibility for how we feel about our world from our own innermost being, our spirit, our soul, and give that power to something that may not be connected to our Beautiful Savior!

This is the power of beatitudes and counting our blessings, and of the entirety of Positive Thinking. Positive thinking is not a means for manipulating the world so that we can have anything we want. These concepts are about using the power of God's Love to connect our souls to the Holy Spirit so through that perfect alignment, our souls are satisfied, and the world receives what it needs to better relate to the Holy Spirit!

As my wife and I walked around our lake this morning, we noticed the trees lining the road; Old Oaks, Maples, Walnut Tree, tall Pines and Spruce. And then there were the flowers, every color and variety. The songbirds sang out their songs, the cardinals, chickadees, warblers, finches, and then the staccato of the woodpeckers after an early morning meal. Past farms grew corn, soybeans, and alfalfa. Along the channel with the bull rushes, cattails, Lilly pads, and fish jumping after dragon flies. A heron swoops in and lands among the cattails hunting for a snack. Beauty at every turn. How many times over the last 50+ years we've walked this path. It never is more beautiful than at the moment you experienced it in the present moment. Being present, now, living each minute as it exists. "But do not overlook this one fact, beloved, that with the Lord one day is as a thousand years, and a thousand years as one day." 2 Peter 3:8 The hidden meaning here is that if we spend our time arguing over what happened a thousand years ago or what will happen over the next thousand years, we miss today, this hour, this minute, and the very second that is now! Everything before this very second is gone and cannot be changed. And the next second is always just that, next; not now but next!

My Prayer: Gracious Creator God, you are timeless. In your presence infinity is nonexistent; for time, space, matter, and energy are irrelevant. If we can measure, describe, assign a beginning or end to you, you are not omniscient, omnipotent, omnipresent, nor are you God! It's time for us to stop arguing and start connecting. The Kingdom is here, within us and each of us holds the key to the door leading to the connection between each of us and the pipeline to the creator. Please remind us of this daily! AMEN

Day 170: A Devotional for Understanding and Acceptance

Yes, I am in favor of all kinds of music. Music has been used for many purposes. Music can connect with the soul. From Ancient times certain tones have been used to soothe and calm the minds of people and others have been used to excite them. It's not just the words but the melodies and harmonies that can generate emotional responses. Aristotle suggested that music could connect the soul to the universe. Tibetan bowls, also known as singing Bowls, have been used as healing devices for centuries. Now, before you say hogwash to all of this, consider research done the Japanese Geneticist, Susumu Ohno, who discovered that DNA patterns were quite musical in nature. When assigned a musical note to correspond to one of the basic nucleotides in DNA, the repetitive nature of the DNA sequence and with its unique variations dependent upon the purpose of a strand created Melodies that can actually be played on modern instruments.

The pitch, tone, volume, and harmonics of an instrument can be used to agitate just as easily as it can be used to calm and please. In fact, some pieces of music have been written to create fear, while others have been written to stimulate peace! There are natural frequencies of the earth, of bridges, of the brain, of the heart, and of everything made up of matter. It is possible to change the rhythm by changing the predominant sounds around a person. As we continue to investigate the impact of music on humanity, we gain clarity of how our world works.

When we consider that the design of life involves an amazing level of interconnection between what we've learned through scientific investigation and naturally occurring phenomena that seem to exist beyond what we know from all the research done to date, it is mind boggling. We've learned so much yet there is still so much more to learn. When we consider the power and intelligence of our Loving God, we realize we've but scratched the surface of what there is to learn!

Our God is an awesome God,

He reigns from heaven above

With wisdom, power, and love

Our God is an awesome God...

Written by Michael W. Smith: 2001

One of the servants answered, "I have seen a son of Jesse of Bethlehem who knows how to play the lyre. He is a brave man and a warrior. He speaks well and is a fine-looking man. And the Lord is with him."

Then Saul sent messengers to Jesse and said, "Send me your son David, who is with the sheep." So, Jesse took a donkey loaded with bread, a skin of wine and a young goat and sent them with his son David to Saul.

David came to Saul and entered his service. Saul liked him very much, and David became one of his armor-bearers. Then Saul sent word to Jesse, saying, "Allow David to remain in my service, for I am pleased with him."

Whenever the spirit from God came on Saul, David would take up his lyre and play. Then relief would come to Saul; he would feel better, and the evil spirit would leave him. 1Samuel 16:18-23

My Prayer: Holy Lord God, bless us with the ability to sooth others through our use of beautiful music. David Played for King Saul and eased his discomfort. We come across so many difficult situations that might be resolved if we would use the calming music that matches the natural frequencies of our lives. Help us to appreciate all the possibilities created in your Universe. Not just the ones that we individually often connect with but also, those musical styles and forms that others find soothing and encouraging. We want to thank you for the variety we can experience, and we want to acknowledge that there are many ways to resolve issues our neighbors face. Help us keep an open mind and let us praise you in all we do. AMEN

Day 171: A Devotional for Understanding and Acceptance

So much of the time it seems like we are in the throes of violent storms or intense heat without rain. During these extreme weather conditions, we all seem to want just a little break. Recently, I've woken up to calm waters, mild breezes, mostly sunny skies, and a single day of gentle rain. This period of a little over a week was a nice respite from the heat, strong winds and thunderstorms we seemed to be experiencing for quite some time. We may return to that weather pattern but while we were blessed with that beautiful weather, parts of Canada were still burning and from Texas to Georgia, they were experiencing extreme heat and almost nightly severe storms with large hail and tornadoes.

We've heard that every dark cloud has its silver lining and perhaps a picture can insert a thousand words here:

This was sunset over Palmer Lake (Colon, MI) on Saturday night. (June17, 2023) The Color of the Sun, as affected by the lingering smoke from the fires in Quebec and Nova Scotia, has not been enhanced or had any special filters applied! That is exactly as we saw it. What an amazingly beautiful sight amidst the horrible tragedy of those fires.

It's very easy to holler at the top of our Lungs that "We are against Climate Change!" Or "We are against the Data Manipulators who want to stifle business growth with their claim that humans caused these natural disasters!" Neither of these approaches have worked yet! They've divided our world into two camps, when God wants us all to join together! Here's something we can all be for!

Let's all declare, that: "We are for all of our people and the places where they live! We know that God Created every person and that God Created every place that people inhabit! We believe every person has the right to live free from serious danger and harm. And to demonstrate that we care, we will share God's Love, Without Conditional Considerations nor strings attached! It's so much better to be for something than to be against the opposite. Being against only requires a sufficient supply of hot air and nastiness! Being for something is about building positive relationships, trust, and creating a vision for the future!

Jesus reminded everyone of the words of Isaiah, when after 40 days in the wilderness, he read scripture in the Synagogue: "The Spirit of the Lord is on me, because he has anointed me to proclaim good news to the poor. He has sent me to proclaim freedom for the prisoners and recovery of sight for the blind, to set the oppressed free, to proclaim the year of the Lord's favor." Luke 4: 18-19 In this he was saying that it was time to stop discriminating against those who suffer; the poor, the imprisoned, and the less able. Jesus clearly told the leaders he confronted that it's not the rules you follow, but the Love and Compassion you show that God wants from us.

My Prayer: Gracious Forgiving God, try as we may, as a group, we humans keep thinking that harsh, disciplined, determined following of all the rules is what you really want! Time and again you show us the errors of our ways, yet we persist. Help us remember that adherence to the letter of the law without Love and the kindness love generates, when analyzed we determine that they are no more helpful than blaring brass, crashing cymbals, or clanging gongs. We are reminded constantly but, in our hearts, we only hear the rules! Teach us to Love as only you and those who deeply love you can Love! AMEN

Day 172: A Devotional for Understanding and Acceptance

For me, finding God's Love in a Grandchild's hug, is one of those things that just create a warm "all over" feeling. Recently My wife and I took our oldest Grandchild, Tessa, on a shopping trip. We had a nice lunch, shopped till we darned near dropped, and the had a delicious Italian Dinner. After getting her back home she gave me one of those hugs that will last me for several days.

Too many people feel, deep inside, that they are not truly worthy. That they need to be punished and that God is just waiting to punish them for all the bad things they've done. And if God decides they aren't going to be punished, they feel they must punish themselves! Nothing could be further from the truth! How do I know this? He would not have sent Jesus to be our Savior! He would not have been willing to let him die the gruesome death on a Cross to Atone for our sins, if he was just waiting to punish us all for our evil nature. God knows we do that to ourselves and we do not need to. We've been redeemed! The price has been paid. Grandchildren know they are loved, and never expect to be punished. Are our Grandchildren perfect? Heaven knows they are not, and we grandparents know they are not, but we love them and would do anything for them!

I think that God must look at all of us like grandchildren. If we would just love God like our grandchildren love us, I truly believe there would be far fewer problems in our world. If we would just all love each other that way. I know my grandparents loved me, and I sure did love them! I know the same could be said for my wife.

Paul tells us to: "Love each other like the members of your family. Be the best at showing honor to each other." ROMANS 12:10 "Little children, let's not love with words or speech but with action and truth." 1 JOHN 3:18 "Be kind, compassionate, and forgiving to each other, in the same way God forgave you in Christ." Ephesians 4:2-3

My Prayer: Gracious Lord, our children and grandchildren need to see our example of love. If we never taught them anything, I think they would still show tremendous love for us. If we show them how much we love them and showed them how much they could help the world by sharing their love, what a difference we could make. There's enough coldness, too much calloused disagreement, and not nearly enough Love. Children know how to love! Let's help them share it wherever they can! AMEN

Day 173: A Devotional for Understanding and Acceptance

We all know them. They are such great friends and when you are putting together a team for any activity or a committee for an organization, we all want to make sure we have one in the mix! These are the People who are always thinking of others! They think of others without even a single thought of "now, they owe me a favor!" This begs the question: Why on earth would anyone want to do that? Being so thoughtful of others without any expectation of getting anything in return!

If you talk to those people, it becomes very obvious. They find incredible joy in doing for others. One close friend of ours is one of these people! She simply says the joy she finds in helping people who feel like; "nobody ever cared one hoot about me, and then you came along and showed me that you cared. It helped to restore my faith in people." That is why they do it! It's not for anything in return, it just feels good to help! They really care about people. They rarely toot their own horn, and even though many people will know someone who fits this description, they will think I'm talking about someone else. Unfortunately, these kind, saintly people often have very few people who will step up and do for them what they do for willingly and lovingly do for others without hesitation. "And as you wish that others would do for you, do so for them." Luke 6:31 "And let us not grow weary of doing good, for in due season we will reap, if we do not give up." Galatians 6:9

My Prayer: Gracious God, protect these wonderful, kind people and give us the presence of mind to honor and support these beautiful souls. Too many of them have been ridiculed by bosses who want them to be more aggressive or even mean. Teach us to be the kind of Christians that want to be exactly what we see here. We need more of these people, and we must realize that the only way to have as many of these saintly people as we need is for each of us to become one! Forget Aggression! Forget Being Mean! Be Kind! Be Humane! Be a Disciple of Christ! AMEN

Day 174: A Devotional for Understanding and Acceptance

One thing that really brings a peaceful feeling to me is working in my vineyard. Vineyards have been around for thousands of years and there are many vineyard references in the Bible. Jesus referred to them in a variety of different parables. One parable is found in Matthew, Mark, and Luke. My vineyard is only 7 rows of vines contained in just a half-acre of land. I don't look at tending my vines as hard work or serious labor. But think about how Jesus used a more commercial approach to "Vineyard Ownership."

And He (Jesus) began to tell the people this parable: "A man planted a vineyard and rented it out to vine-growers and went on a journey for a long time. At harvest time he sent a slave to the vine-growers, so that they would give him some of the produce of the vineyard; but the vine-growers beat him and sent him away empty-handed. And he proceeded to send another slave; and they beat him also and treated him shamefully and sent him away empty-handed. And he proceeded to send a third; and this one also they wounded and cast out. The owner of the vineyard said, 'What shall I do? I will send my beloved Son; perhaps they will respect him.' But when the vine-growers saw him, they reasoned with one another, saying, 'This is the heir; let us kill him so that the inheritance will be ours.' So, they threw him out of the vineyard and killed him. What, then, will the owner of the  vineyard do to them? He will come and destroy these vine-growers and will give the vineyard to others." When they heard it, they said, "May it never be!" But Jesus looked at them and said, "What then is this that is written. The stone which the builders rejected became the chief corner stone'? Everyone who falls on that stone will be broken to pieces; but on whomever it falls, it will scatter him like dust." (Luke 20:9-18) This story is also told in Mark 12:1-11 and Matthew 21:33-44 This is consistent and verification of this as a key message from our savior and is told so that we will realize that what we are called to do, on behalf of our God, is always have our first fruits going to support the Lord's work. Should we deny that we are rejecting Christ and the spirit of our Living God! My vineyard work is in this beautiful scenic vineyard in the lots across the street from our house. For me this work, as well as all work I do for the glory of our God! "Then sings my soul- My Savior God to thee- How Great Thou Art!"

My Prayer: Glorious Savior God, Savior Son, and Savior Spirit: Bless All who do the work of expanding Christ's discipleship throughout our world. We pray a healing spirit will fall upon and heal all who are suffering from any affliction that is challenging them at this time. I want to specifically ask for your healing blessing on the people I bring to you at this moment! (Tell the Devine Spirit the name of people you desire to be healed) We truly believe if we come to you, Gracious Lord of All, healing will just take place. Thank You AMEN

Day 175: A Devotional for Understanding and Acceptance

We often think that a person's talent is pretty much set by the time they reach adulthood. I have very solid evidence that this could not be further from the truth when looking at my mother's watercolor paintings. My started painting when she was 60 years old. After my dad died in 1989, my mom started looking for new activities that would expand her horizons. She took up photography and took some amazing pictures. And then she decided to try her hand at painting. Over the next 20 years she constantly had her easels set up and had at least two pictures in progress.

It was not that my dad kept my mom from exploring her talents, but when he died my mom had to figure out everything for herself. In that process, she had to become her own advocate and advisor. She read books and took classes and decided she needed to sell the 5 bedroom house that had been her dream house. My mom lived there from 1964 until 1990 and if she was going to sell it, she might as well relocate to Minnesota where she could be closer to her aging parents. She didn't ask my two brothers and I for input. She told us she was selling her house and was going to move to the suburbs of Minneapolis. She was going to help Uncle Jack take care of Grandma and Grandpa Shobe. So, she sold her house, hired a mover, and bought a 2 bedroom condo in Burnsville, MN! After 25 years in Mt. Prospect, she stated her intention to move to Minnesota and that's just what she did!

I've recently been exploring how people truly get closer to their divine nature. There are several great thinkers that have documented what they believe are key points in the individual's journey towards a more intimate relationship with our Creator. In nearly all the writings I've come across, the very first step is to be intentional! The power of intentionality coupled with God's grace puts us on a trajectory for discovering the greater depths of our souls. That was where my mom began her journey after deciding to leave the Chicagoland area, late in 1990. She proved that it is never too late to be intentional about your life. The painting below was one of the wonderful gifts my mom left me.

"Every good and perfect gift is from above, coming down from the Father of the heavenly lights, who does not change like shifting shadows." James 1:17

"There are different kinds of gifts, but the same Spirit distributes them. There are different kinds of service, but the same Lord. There are different kinds of working, but in all of them and in everyone it is the same God at work." 1 Corinthians 12: 4-6

My Prayer: Gracious Creator God, I ask that you teach us all these amazing steps towards a closer walk with you. Let us:

1. Be intentional in our seeking of a better future for ourselves and our loved ones and always within the bounds of Your grace.
2. Be Kind to everyone as we know kindness is essential and reflects how you would want us to treaty one another.
3. Be the love you ask us to share, knowing love is the force behind our Creative/Creator God!
4. Be Beauty so that we might have the capacity to create beauty, whether that beauty is of an artistic nature or a beautiful spirit.
5. Be expansive for nothing that pertains to our Amazing Creator God can be contained with the limitations of a box

6. Be abundant for there is never any chance of not having enough when we are in God's Presence

7. Be Receptive for the only reason we ever feel we are in want of anything is based on our failure to recognize the astounding gifts God is ready to pour out on us.

We ask this in the name of Your son, our beloved Savior Jesus, and the Holy Spirit who guides us, and of course your precious Name I Am. AMEN

Day 176: A Devotional for Understanding and Acceptance

The Independence Day Holiday is fast approaching. The warmest part of summer is just around the meteorological corner, so to speak. It's these warm days of summer that make me truly appreciate the beautiful shade trees. The Oak and Maple trees in our yard shade our home and keep the sweltering sun from heating it to beyond the point at which comfort is nearly unattainable. In days long since passed, before almost every home had air conditioning, the coolness of the shade and a gentle breeze was about as good as it got during summer. We did without central air conditioning until our present reconfiguration of our home in Michigan was completed in 2011. Shade and a breeze off the lake was nature's way of keeping us cool at night. During the day was an entirely different situation, but we managed.

The idea of taking comfort from the shade of the old maple and oak trees that shaded our home and the coolness of the breeze blowing in from the lake reminds of one of my favorite Bible verses; "I am the vine; you are the branches. If you remain in me and I in you, you will bear much fruit; apart from me you can do nothing." John 15:5 Although, Jesus, is talking about our personal relationship with him and through him to our Great Lord God, Creator of all that is, it is comforting to think that we are part of the same living system as Jesus and the Creator. As long as we remain faithful to our trees and care for them, they will be of service to us. Similarly, as long as we remain faithful in our relationship with God, he will always be faithful to us!

My Prayer: Gracious God, thank you for Loving and caring for us. You are the Great I Am. There can be no peace or joy in this world unless we, your Creation, bring it forth. You have provided the means, the resources, the tools, and the directions to accomplish this. It's up to us to make it happen! We must be Christ's feet, legs, arms, hands and voice! So many people are counting on us to help them find their way. We must remain in Jesus and allow Jesus to remain in us, and we will find that Beautiful Shade Tree where we can all find respite from the heat of our times! AMEN

Day 177: A Devotional for Understanding and Acceptance

What could be more satisfying than the sound of laughter after a long day of stressful of dealing

with problems you'd rather not had to deal with? We often think of our Lord Jesus as having a solemn, almost brooding, Saintly appearance. Many years ago, there was drawing of "Jesus Laughing." While I was going through my new membership classes to become a member of the Arlington Heights First United Methodist Church, I came across this drawing and framed it for my home.

I've always loved that image of Christ. It didn't make sense to me that Jesus would ask us to be joyful, yet he never was depicted having the same joy we were expected to have. So when I found that picture, I had to frame it and hang it on my wall. "Blessed are you who hunger now, for you will be satisfied. Blessed are you who weep now, for you will laugh." Luke 6:21

As rain will end a drought's withering of crops, gardens, lawns, and flower beds, so will laughter end our sorrows, disappointments, and frustrations. Do not give in to the difficulties of these times. Do not fear the future, for our future will be what we make it. God will give us the future we desire, if we only show to the world our faith that God will deliver it to us. We cannot show the world our faith through doubt, sadness, and despair. Having faith is believing it is already ours, even before it has arrived. Too many of us have more faith in Amazon and FedEx than we do our God. "Therefore, I tell you, do not worry about your life, what you will eat or drink; or about your body, what you will wear. Is not life more than food, and the body more than clothes? Look at the birds of the air; they do not sow or reap or store away in barns, and yet your heavenly Father feeds them.

Are you not much more valuable than they? Can any one of you by worrying add a single hour to your life? Matthew 6:25-27

My Prayer: Beautiful Savior, help us! We say we have faith but are full of doubt and fear. In this doubt and fear, we do things you would never have us do. We put twists on your words you would never do yourself and I see us heading in a direction that is far from the Love you've commanded us to share. Show us how to Love First, Forgive Second, and under no circumstance promote hate and disgust. You have brought joy and release from bondage to our hearts. Help us do the same for every other person we meet. We pray this in your name and in the name of your loving father. AMEN

Day 178: A Devotional for Understanding and Acceptance

There are so many things in today's world that only serve to bring us down. If we give in to them, we can make ourselves miserable. We can find some bad in every experience. As we look at the work done in any situation, we can find fault. We all need an event or activity that allows us a respite from our constant desire to explore the depths of what's wrong with the world today. One very transformative and positive building activity for me is walking in the country with my wife.

We've found some marvelous walking trails in our own county, and these show us amazing beauty. It would be easy to interpret what we have come across as flawed. There are trees that have been blown over by storms that if in my yard it would require immediate clean-up work which would have me focusing on climate change or other issues impacting our world. But in these surroundings, we see how it is necessary to the cycle of life. Without some trees falling in the woods, organisms that need the nutrients from that tree might not get their nutrients. It becomes obvious that nothing is truly random, it's all part of a greater plan.

We all need those places we can go and leave our troubles behind, even if we find them as soon as we are back. But, as we face our challenges with a clearer head, we just might see things with a little positive view. It's meditation on the move! We can't always get away from it all but we can allow our minds some space with a quiet walk through some beautiful scenery. "Let the peace of Christ rule in your hearts, since as members of one body you were called to peace. And be thankful." Colossians: 3:15

My Prayer: Savior Jesus, help us put our troubles into perspective. We too often feel as though the weight of the world is on our backs, but you have told us to see things differently. You've said to us: "Come to me, all you who are weary and burdened, and I will give you rest. Take my yoke upon you and learn from me, for I am gentle and humble in heart, and you will find rest for your souls. For my yoke is easy and my burden is light." Matthew 11:28-30 help us remind and buoy each other up as we hit those rough patches. We do, indeed, place our trust in you but we need to be nudged and reminded. We are blessed to be Christians and live in your eternal favor. AMEN

Day 179: A Devotional for Understanding and Acceptance

I was in the Chicago area recently, and I was reminded, very quickly, of the difference between rural America and urban America. It's not hard to pick out the differences. It used to be considerably easier as there was a certain speed gap between the two; the speed at which traffic moves, and just the speed of life in general. Also, the clothing, hair styles, and language were considerably different. Today, with mass media, the internet and social media, many things are coming closer together. But there are still some very big differences.

The number of people per square mile. The number and height of buildings. The amount if traffic and the number of highways all going somewhere or coming from somewhere. In our little town of Colon, Michigan there's only one State highway running through it and only a blinker light marking the 4 way stop Downtown. I enjoy my small town, but I also enjoy the big city.

It's not probable that we would see a lone violinist playing haunting Melodies when you are not expecting it in my town. But in the big city, I've seen that more than a dozen times. In the big city, it is highly unlikely that a secondary street will have a combine blocking traffic, but that's commonplace in rural areas. Big cities and rural towns are not opposites, they exist in entirely different ideas in the minds of humans. There are cities that seem big but are really just large, small towns. And there are small towns that are really just small cities. It's more about how the people in those municipalities see themselves and less about the population.

In a very comparable way, there is no opposite of love! You can experience a little love or a whole lot of love. Hate is on a spectrum all of its own! It is not the opposite of love. It is true that people who hate seem to have great difficulty loving people but it's not impossible. It's truly about your perspective and what you are willing to let yourself feel. Jesus disciples knew this about people and told us so many times.

Love "bears all things, believes all things, hopes all things, endures all things. Love never fails. " 1 Corinthians 13:8

Love is patient, love is kind. It does not envy, it does not boast, it is not proud. It does not dishonor others, it is not self-seeking, it is not easily angered, it keeps no record of wrongs. 1 Corinthians 13:4-5.

My Prayer: Gracious God, we know that we see differences in our world. Big and small, rich and poor, happy and sad, satisfied and dissatisfied. But we also know these are not permanent circumstances. Any situation or circumstance can change. It becomes easier for us to change when we stop looking at situations or events as being either or. In your Creation all things are possible, and we need only believe to make what we desire into a reality. It's not about how worthy anyone is, because we all fall short of the perfection that is our goal. However, with your help and guidance and through our deep faith, we will show you what we can do on your behalf, and we will be able to apply your bountiful gifts to advance the work of your beautiful Savior Son, our Loving Jesus. Love has been a constant theme and we all certainly hope we are learning how to love more, care better, and live the faith filled life you've asked us to live. Thank you for your patience! AMEN

Day 180: A Devotional for Understanding and Acceptance

For the past few days, as I've looked outside, I've seen a haze over the entire area. There have been Wildfires raging in Canada. Dry and excessively warm conditions have resulted in over 19 million acres of Canadian Forests having been burned. Today, there are 490 separate active fires in Canada with the closest fire to Kalamazoo, Michigan (the closest metropolitan area to my home) still over 300 miles away. Yet, our air quality is the unhealthy for sensitive groups level. Yesterday it was in the seriously bad region, like don't go outside bad for our area.

When it's hard to breathe due to air quality, one begins to wonder is there anything we can do to improve the environment and reduce the chances of these raging fires. They've become commonplace around the world; from grass fires in Australia, parts of Asia, and Africa, to forest fires in the Europe, the northern US and Canada, and even the swamps in Florida and the Amazon Rain Forests in Brazil have dried up at various times and caught fire. What's our world to do?

One thing is for certain, when we argue over the causes of our current problems, and who's to blame, rather than put our minds on finding solutions, everybody loses. "Brothers, I do not consider that I have made it my own. But one thing I do: forgetting what lies behind (what happened in the past) and straining forward to what lies ahead (our promised future), I press on toward the goal for the prize of the upward call of God in Christ Jesus." Philippians 3: 13-14

My Prayer: Holy God, Lord of Life, we pray that all of your children will learn to cooperate on finding real solutions to our greatest problems. The environmental catastrophe of forest and grassland fires, shortages of medications for cancer treatments and diabetes mitigation, gun related deaths, and disregard for basic human rights in many different countries around the world, both by governments and private citizens; all of these are taxing the patience of loving Christians everywhere. We need a tsunami of "continuous, intensive prayers of love and care" for all of the people who have been, are being, or could be harmed by this chaos. Lord God of All, we are willing to get this cause moving forward. We are not completely certain of everything we will need to do to cause this to happen, but we eagerly await the inspiration from your Holy Spirit to advance this cause! Once again, we thank you for your Love, Patience, and Guidance! AMEN

Day 181: A Devotional for Understanding and Acceptance:

"Where, O death, is your victory? Where, O death, is your sting?" The sting of death is sin, and the power of sin is the law. But thanks be to God! He gives us the victory through our Lord Jesus Christ. 1 Corinthians 15: 55-57

In a week's time, we attended 3 funeral services. In each one, this verse was read. I'm of a mind to consider death just as any other transition in life. We begin as a twinkle in our parents' eyes, and then if all goes as planned, we become an embryo, then a fetus, and finally we exit the comfort of the womb and enter to cold reality of our temporal life. We transition from a temporal baby to a temporal infant, to child, teen, adult, and eventually we exit this temporal existence and transition to a spiritual existence. But my question is, why wait? You do not have to die "your physical death" to experience "your spiritual life!" Granted, most people are too busy with their "stuff and things" or their "things and stuff," to "waste their time" on experiencing their "spiritual lives!" But what could be more amazing than to connect with God on a very spiritual level?

We all have the capacity to do this. I have done so, and first did at age 16. I was late in my introduction to Jesus. My parents were from 2 different church traditions and decided to let us kids each figure out what we wanted to be. The summer before I entered High School a friend invited me to attend a Young Life Meeting. The Leader was a math teacher at the High School I was going to attend. I was amazed at what I heard and felt something different inside. I knew about Christmas and Easter, but only slightly more than Christmas presents and Easter Egg hunts. Mr. Ecker, the YL Leader helped to open my eyes to what it meant to be a Christian.

At 16 I had my first experience with my inner spirit connecting with what I believe was the Holy Spirit, who walked with me, not a physical presence but a truly warm comforting presence on a cool morning, the day after my grandfather died. He had lived with us for 3 years, since my grandmother passed. I spent many an afternoon sitting by his side, asking him questions, and listening to him explain things and I received an amazing gift. My grandfather told me stories about his life he never even shared with my dad. After he died, I went for a walk in the cool of the morning feeling awful. Knowing there was so much more I could learn from him and knowing I'd never be able to talk to him again as I walked, I felt a presence that truly changed everything. After that morning walk, I went home and took out my newest guitar, a Gibson B25-12 String with a

Sunburst front and wrote a Song. I played that Song for the Young Life Group, and from what I've heard, that song may still be part of the Young Life Song Book. I've made a few changes over the years, but for some reason, perhaps I was worried about people thinking I was truly weird, I have never shared the original source for the song. Now everyone knows "The Rest of the Story;" to steal an idea from Paul Harvey.

My Prayer is that Song I wrote in 1966: **Before I Walked With Jesus:**

 1st verse: Before I walked with Jesus My feet moved but I went nowhere

Before I walked with Jesus I had so little to share

But now I walk with Jesus With Purpose and focused eye

I know just where I'm going And Jesus is the reason Why!

Chorus:

Don't wait till it's too late Let Jesus have your heart

There's no reason to deny him He forgave us all our sins

Don't wait until tomorrow, Tomorrow never comes

Give your heart away to Jesus The battles already won

2nd Verse: Before I talked with Jesus I spoke too much each day

Before I talked with Jesus I had so little to say

But now I talk with Jesus No problem he won't solve

Now I talk with Jesus My Savior I do resolve

Chorus

Don't wait till it's too late Let Jesus have your heart

There's no reason to deny him He forgave us all our sins

Don't wait until tomorrow, Tomorrow never comes

Give your heart away to Jesus The battles already won

3rd verse: Before I saw Jesus I thought I was in Control

Before I saw Jesus I thought I knew it all

But now that I see Jesus Here inside of me

I can feel all my tomorrows Will be the best day ever for me

Chorus:

Don't wait till it's too late Let Jesus have your heart

There's no reason to deny him He forgave us all our sins

Don't wait until tomorrow, Tomorrow never comes

Give your heart away to Jesus The battles already won

Repeat last 2 lines

AMEN HALLELUJAH AMEN

I could not write this without tears! I SAY AGAIN HALLELUJAH AMEN

Day 182: A Devotional for Understanding and Acceptance:

We are at the halfway point of the year. It's July 1st and month wise, there are 6 months to New Years Eve. That will mark the time to celebrate the past year in anticipation of the New Year. A time to reminisce with family and friends about the glorious fun we had during so many visits and trips and just being together! During these last 6 months of 2024, let's dedicate our time and energy to focusing on the world we do want! Where we put our focus will be the experience we have. If we focus on trying to stop all the things we don't want, you can "bet your sweet bippy" that you just get more or what you don't want! (a reference "you bet your bippy" from Dan Rowan and Dick Martin's TV Program Laugh In: 1968-1973)

So, I say, let's focus on what we do want. Here's one thing I'd really like to see in place for 2024! A campaign season that is highlighted by decency, civility, integrity, and kindness. Oh, there's no doubt that things will be said, and accusations will be made, but we the American People, have a choice we can make in every situation. We can choose to be kind, or we can choose to get into the arguments, and verbal brawls (which from time to time have actually resulted in physical acts of violence) that have become all too common is the elections in the United States. I can hear some people saying, right now, that you expect us to just sit there and take the verbal abuse and insults and not fight back! That's crazy!

Consider this old story from many, many centuries ago. It seems that one of the wisest teachers of a particular region was known for the incredible advice he gave to people. One day, one of the people who had received his advice, tried to apply what he had been advised to do, however, he was not very patient and did not continue following the advice for the prescribed period of time and everything went from bad to worse. This young man go so angry, he went to that wise old teacher, and berated him. He called every horrible name that he could think of and hurled every insult he could come up with. The wise old teacher just sat with the slightest hint of a smile on his face. When the young man's tirade finally ended, the wise old teacher simply smiled and said "thank you for presenting me with this gift." The young man was in shock. He looked at his teacher and said, "you crazy old fool, I didn't give a gift; I gave you a tongue lashing and used every insult I could think of!" The wise old teacher said, "what do you call something that someone gives you? Isn't it a gift, something that someone gives you? Now tell me, if the receiver of a gift, refuses to accept the gift, who does that gift belong to?" The young man said, "why the gift giver, I suppose." "Well," the wise old teacher said, I am refusing to accept your gift. Thank you very much for my critique, but I would not know what to do with all you said. So, in all kindness, I must refuse your gift!" Finally, the young man understood! He had tears in his eyes when finally said to the teacher: "I accept your gift! I don't know how I can ever repay you for this lesson and your kindness." The teacher said, "You just did!" And his student wept!

In every circumstance we find ourselves with one of two choices. We can choose to do things the way the world expects us to do things, or we can choose the way of The Christ! That way can only be Kindness and Love! "Do not let any unwholesome talk come out of your mouths, but only what is helpful for building others up according to their needs, that it may benefit those who listen." Ephesians 4:29 "Therefore, as God's chosen people, holy and dearly loved, clothe yourselves with compassion, kindness, humility, gentleness and patience." Colossians 3:12 "But the fruit of the Spirit is love, joy, peace, forbearance, kindness, goodness, faithfulness, gentleness and self-control. Against such things, there is no Law." Galatians 5:22

My Prayer: Gracious God, let us all follow the teaching of Paul the Apostle. He very clearly would find today's political climate very unsavory and would rebuke most politicians in almost every race. We a have Avery clear choice! If we support a candidate, please ask them to maintain civility and above all else, be kind! Jesus told us to "Live our Enemies!" Not just the people agree with us, like us, and are in our circle of friends. As Jesus told us, Don't the Unbelievers do that as well? If we are to separate ourselves from the masses of people who are more concerned with material world than they are aligning themselves with the Commands that Jesus gave us, what improvements are we really liking for? Help us find clarity in your teaching! Help us to align with what truly want us to be! Help get our spiritual inner selves into synchronicity with the Holy Spirit! That is how we will let the world we are Christians because our inner spiritual selves are fully aligned, all that will remain is the Unconditional Love Christ had asked us to share! AMEN

Printed in the USA
CPSIA information can be obtained
at www.ICGtesting.com
JSHW05232503072 4
65791JS00002B/3

9 798869 325433